Stained Glass
Projects & Patterns

George Shannon & Pat Torlen

Sterling Publishing Co., Inc.   New York
A STERLING/TAMOS BOOK

For Elizabeth Shannon

**Special thanks to
Amy Irwin, Wendy Meyer,
Judy Sharratt, and
Brianna Stark**

A Sterling/Tamos Book
© George W. Shannon and Pat Torlen
Glass project designs/patterns © G. W. Shannon
and P. Torlen

Sterling Publishing Co., Inc.
387 Park Avenue South, New York, NY 10016 8810

TAMOS Books Inc.
300 Wales Avenue, Winnipeg, MB, Canada R2M 2S9

10 9 8 7 5 4 3 2 1

Distributed in Canada by Sterling Publishing Co., Inc.
c/o Canadian Manda Group, One Atlantic Avenue, Suite 105
Toronto, Ontario, Canada M6K 3E7
Distributed in Great Britain and Europe by Cassell PLC,
Wellington House, 125 Strand, London WC2R 0BB, England
Distributed in Australia by Capricorn Link (Australia) Pty Ltd.
P.O. Box 6651, Baulkham Hills, Business Centre, NSW 2153,
Australia

Design Arlene Osen
Photography Jerry Grajewski, Custom Images Ltd.
Printed in China

Canadian Cataloging-in-Publication Data
Shannon, George W. (George Wylie), 1961–
     Stained glass
     "A Sterling/Tamos book."
     Includes index.
     ISBN 1-895569-40-0
1. Glass craft. 2. Glass painting and staining.
I. Torlen, Patricia, 1960– II. Title.
TT298.S435 1995   748.5'028   C95-920101-7

Library of Congress Cataloging-in-Publication Data
Shannon, George (George Wylie), 1961–
     Stained glass: projects & patterns/by George Shannon
  & Pat Torlen.
          p.   cm.
     "A Sterling/Tamos book."
     Includes index.
     ISBN 1-895569-40-0
     1. Glass painting and staining–Patterns. I. Torlen, Pat,
  1960–. II. Title.
TT298.S44 1995   95–34184
748.5'028–dc20   CIP

ISBN 1-895569-40-0

NOTE Because of the lead solder these projects are not suitable for holding food. Also since solder seams may leak, vases should be used only for dried flowers. If you wish to use fresh flowers insert a plastic container to hold the water.

NOTE If you prefer to work in metric measurements, to convert inches to millimeters multiply by 25.4.

NOTE Copper foil stained glass construction projects are not recommended for children under age 12. Because of safety factors when cutting glass and soldering, ages 12 to 16 should have adult supervision when working on projects in this book.

The advice and directions given in this book have been carefully checked, prior to printing, by the Author as well as the Publisher. Nevertheless, no guarantee can be given as to project outcome due to the possible differences in materials and the Author and Publisher will not be responsible for the results.

Table of Contents

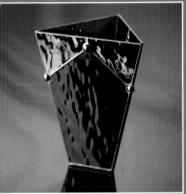

Introduction

Brilliant hues and sparkling bevels immediately identify traditional stained glass, a beautiful and fashionable art to adorn houses of worship, commercial buildings, and homes. The unique effect of stained glass is created when light plays on the dazzling mosaic of individual pieces of richly colored art glass pieced together into intricate designs. The finished piece can be simple or complex. Its various textures and surfaces, its shape and outline are created for all to enjoy.

Once the sole domain of teams of skilled craftsmen producing pictorial windows for churches and elaborate homes, stained glass has undergone an incredible evolution in the past century. Since the resurgence of the arts and crafts movement in the 1970s, hobbyists have embraced this dynamic medium in ever increasing numbers. With the development of new and better equipment and access to an increasing array of materials, stained glass construction has never been easier or more affordable.

This hobby can now be enjoyed by everyone. All it takes is a little time and practice to master the techniques involved. Use this book as your guide. Original contemporary stained glass patterns are supplied with step-by-step instructions and pictures to guide the novice through each stage required in the copper foil construction technique. This technique, first associated with Louis Comfort Tiffany, is the most popular method used by hobbyists because of the intricate detail that can be achieved and the variety of projects that can be made. By following the step-by-step instructions demonstrated throughout, hobbyists will be able to master the use of the tools and skills involved to complete the projects of their choice. Additional patterns, for all skill levels, are included and incorporate some different techniques to add interest to your project. Contemporary stained glass is an ideal craft for anyone wishing to express themselves in creative and imaginative ways.

Glass

Glass is not a naturally occurring substance. It is formed when quantities of silica, sand, soda ash, and lime are heated in a furnace to a molten state at a temperature in excess of 2000°F. Colors are produced by adding metal oxides to the molten batch. Cobalt and chromium produce blue, add manganese to cobalt blue for purple, add copper for greens and blacks, selenium and cadmium for red and yellow, and gold oxides for gold-pinks. Sheets of stained glass are then produced using one of three methods: mouth-blown antique, machine rolled, or hand cast.

Some of the most beautiful sheets of stained glass are produced by using the traditional technique of mouth blowing. Teams of glassblowers pick molten glass up out of the furnace on the end of a blow pipe. A cylindrical shape is blown and then rotated in a mold to even the surface and create striations unique to antique glass. The ends are cut off and the cylinder is cut lengthwise and allowed to flatten and form a sheet of glass. The sheet is then gradually cooled in a large temperature-controlled oven, called a lehr. This process, called annealing, allows the sheets of glass to cool at a controlled rate to relieve unwanted stress within the glass. The cutability of a glass is usually determined in the annealing stage. Rich, translucent hues are characteristic of glass made using this early method of glassmaking.

Machine-rolled glass is known for its consistency in color and thickness and is generally easier to cut. Molten glass is continuously fed through sets of metal rollers and onto a slow-moving conveyer-type line. As the glass passes through the roller, patterns and textures can be embossed on the surface before the ribbon of glass reaches the lehr.

Hand-cast glass is produced one sheet at a time. Using a large ladle, molten glass is poured onto a metal table and rolled by hand to the desired thickness. Interesting sheets of glass can be produced by mixing in swirls of different colors, thin glass rods, and shards of colored glass before the sheet of glass is transferred to the lehr and allowed to gradually cool.

Glass Types—Quality art glasses in exciting colors and textures are available in sheets. Choose from

FULL ANTIQUE A traditional mouth-blown glass characterized by rich coloring, translucence, and surface striations. This glass is not always uniform in thickness and color shading. Trapped air bubbles and pockets, which appear due to the blowing process, also add interest.

SEMI-ANTIQUE Machine-made, semi-antique glass is translucent, of a single uniform color, consistent thickness, and has surface striations. Air bubbles are not present in semi-antique glass.

CATHEDRAL Translucent and usually of a single color, cathedral glass is reminiscent of the glass traditionally used in making church windows. It can be machine-rolled or mouth-blown.

OPALESCENT Often milky in appearance, opalescent glass can be a single color or a combination of two or more colors swirled together. It is opaque, transmits little light, and its colors are best seen in reflected light. It can be machine-rolled or hand cast. Each sheet has varying color patterns and can be embossed with textures on one side. These glasses are used frequently for constructing lamp shades.

FLASHED This form of antique glass has a thin layer of a second color on top of the base color. Portions of the base layer can be exposed by sandblasting or acid etching away parts of the top layer, creating tremendous detail.

GLUE CHIP The process of glue chipping creates effects like patterns of frost on a window. Animal hide glue is applied to cathedral glass that has been sandblasted. As the glue dries, it tears away flakes of glass from the sheet's surface, creating a pattern.

CRAQUEL The craquel effect (an alligator-like pattern on one side) is produced by dipping antique glass in water during the initial stages of manufacturing. Craquel glass is made in translucent colors only. It is best used as an accent.

RING MOTTLED This is a hand cast opalescent glass with a hazy surface covering small circular patterns within the glass. It is used for tiffany-style lamp shades and window panels.

FRACTURES AND STREAMERS Known as "confetti" glass, this hand-cast glass is created by adding elements to a clear or opalescent base sheet. It can be used to represent distant foliage or to add interest to a contemporary design.

STREAKY Streaky glasses are swirls of two or more colors mixed but not blended together.

SEEDY This cathedral glass with a smooth surface has small air bubbles dispersed throughout.

IRIDESCENT A shimmering rainbow-like finish can be created on cathedral or opalescent glass by coating the surface with an ultra-thin layer of metallic salts during the manufacturing process.

REAMY An antique glass characterized by uneven ridges and handmade appearance.

DRAPERY This glass contains deep ridges and valleys throughout.

TEXTURED Ripple, hammered, granite, crystal ice, herringbone, fibroid, florentine, moss, flemish, muffle, and cube are just a few of the textures available.

BEVELS A piece of glass is cut to the shape required and an angled border of approximately 1/2 in wide is ground and polished on the topside edges of the piece. When light strikes the beveled edges, it refracts and sends rainbows of color throughout a room. Individual beveled pieces or clusters can be purchased in a wide variety of shapes and sizes. Bevels are often used in traditional stained glass window panels, French doors, and as an accent in lamp shades and contemporary designs.

JEWELS These pieces of glass are often faceted and come in a selection of shapes and colors. They can be used in making windows, jewelry, or to highlight any stained glass piece.

GLASS GLOBS OR NUGGETS Irregular in shape and size, these are used in much the same manner as glass jewels.

RONDELS These are circles made of spun glass. They are usually translucent and are available in a variety of sizes and colors.

Copper Foil Construction

Various materials and tools commonly found around the home can be used for copper foil construction of stained glass projects. As well you'll need some equipment specifically designed for stained glass construction. Most urban centers have at least one retail outlet that caters to stained glass craftsmen and several companies offer a mail order service. Check your telephone directory yellow pages for a listing of local shops and establishments offering mail order service. If you know someone who has worked with stained glass, ask them for recommendations. There is a wide selection of tools and materials available. Finding the tool that best suits your needs or that special piece of stained glass to complete any project in this book should not be difficult.

Materials

COPPER FOIL   Copper foil supplies the base from which the metal support structure is created to join together the pieces of glass in a stained glass project. An adhesive-backed copper foil tape is wrapped around each piece of glass once it has been cut and ground to shape. Molten solder is then applied with a soldering iron along the foiled seam that is created when the individual foiled glass pieces are placed side by side on the pattern. The rounded solder seams hold the pieces of stained glass in place. Copper foil is available in rolls 36 yards long from 1/8 in to 12 in wide. The most common foils used are 3/16 in to 1/4 in wide, depending on the thickness of the glass used. Copper foil also comes in 12-in square sheets that are used primarily for creating decorative overlays. Copper foil with a silver or black backing can be used when the glass is translucent and a view of the copper is not desired.

FLUX   Before a stained glass project can be soldered together, the copper foil must be clean and free of oxidation to ensure an even solder seam. The application of flux aids in the fusion of the solder to the copper foil. Solder will not stick to the copper foil if flux is not applied. Flux solutions are available in a variety of forms—paste, gel, liquid, or cream. A water-soluble safety flux formulated for stained glass construction is recommended. Fluxes containing zinc chloride and hydrochloric acids should be avoided because they can cause skin and respiratory irritations in some individuals.

SOLDER   Solder is an alloy composed primarily of tin and lead that will fuse to the copper foil when heat is applied (approximately 600 to 800°F). For ease in handling, solder is produced as a solid wire, approximately 1/8 in thick, and comes in one-pound spools. The most commonly used solders for copper foil construction are

60/40–combination of 60% tin and 40% lead. It melts quickly and is easy to work with when trying to achieve a rounded solder seam. Once it cools, the surface has a shiny finish.

50/50–equal parts of tin and lead. This solder melts at a higher temperature and takes longer to solidify. It is often used as a basecoat on the seams of 3-dimensional objects to help prevent the final bead of solder from melting through seams.

Lead free–consists primarily of tin and is recommended for the construction of stained glass jewelry and any project where lead content is a concern. Its melting point is higher than the other 2 solders making it more difficult to work with.

On labels, the amount of tin present in a spool of solder is listed first, followed by the lead content.

CAME   Extruded lengths of channeled metal used to hold pieces of stained glass together are called "came." H-shaped lengths of lead were used in the tenth century to build some of the first stained glass windows and are still used today. U-shaped cames are used to finish the outside border of a project. Came is available in lengths of approximately 6 feet and is also manufactured in zinc, brass, and copper.

VASE CAPS AND SPIDERS   A vase cap is usually made of spun brass, is circular in shape, and should have several small vent holes to let the heat escape that is given off by the light bulb. It is soldered over the top opening of the lamp shade and assists in holding the individual panels of the shade together. A small brass ring with 3 or 4 spoke-like arms radiating outward is called a spider. It is used in lamp shades when covering the top opening is not desired. It can be used in conjunction with a vase cap to lend additional support on large lamp shades. Both are used to give the lamp shade support and a means to suspend it from a ceiling fixture or on a lamp base.

HINGE AND FINE-LINK CHAIN   A brass tube and the rod that fits within it can create a hinge for the lid of a stained glass box. One end of a fine-link chain can be attached to the lid and the other end secured to the bottom of the box to prevent the lid from flopping over and breaking.

TINNED COPPER WIRE   18 to 20 gauge copper wire can be purchased with or without a slight coating of tin. Tinned copper wire is used to add strength and as a finishing border around lamp shades and small window panels. Copper wire can be tinned by applying flux and thinly coating the wire with solder.

LUBRICANT   A lubricant is required to keep the wheel of the glass cutter clean and well oiled. Kerosene is still used but there are other types of lightweight oil available that are odorless and water soluble.

PATINA   This solution of water, copper sulfates, and mineral acids is applied to a solder seam to change the surface of the solder to a copper or black finish.

NEUTRALIZING SOLUTION A neutralizing solution of water, sodium bicarbonate, and detergent is used to wash off all traces of flux and patina when a stained glass project is completed.

FINISHING WAX A wax compound applied to the solder seams of all finished stained glass projects can be buffed with a soft cloth, leaving seams shiny and with a protective coating. Specially formulated stained glass finishing compounds or a quality car wax can be used.

Equipment

PERMANENT WATERPROOF FINE-TIPPED MARKER This tool is used for outlining the pattern pieces on the glass during the cutting and grinding stages. For dark and opaque glasses, a silver marker is ideal.

DRAFTING EQUIPMENT –*small square, pencil, cork-backed straightedge, grid paper, tracing paper, light cardstock* Drafting materials and tools assist in making copies of patterns, in scoring and cutting straight lines, verifying angles and proper alignment, and are used to make templates.

GLASS CUTTERS These are needed to accurately score and break individual pieces of glass to fit the project pattern. The two most common types of glass cutters are dry wheel and oil-fed. An inexpensive steel wheel cutter has a larger steel cutting wheel and is usually disposed of after each project. A lubricant must be applied to the steel wheel before each score is made. In comparison, self-lubricating cutters, which have smaller cutting wheels made of carbide steel and a reservoir for oil, are more expensive but last for many years. The smaller sized wheel can better follow the contours and uneven surfaces of art glass and is therefore preferred. Popular models have either a traditional pencil-shaped barrel or a pistol grip handle. The pistol grip handle is advantageous for people with limited strength in their hands and for reducing fatigue when scoring glass.

BREAKING/GROZING PLIERS Breaking pliers have flat smooth jaws that are well suited for gripping and breaking off scored pieces of glass. Grozing pliers have narrow, flat, serrated jaws to nibble away at unwanted bits along the edge of the cut glass so the piece will fit the pattern. Glass grinders greatly reduce the need for grozing pliers. Combination pliers combine the uses of breaking and grozing pliers. The top jaw is flat and the bottom jaw is concave–both are serrated. These are the most popular pliers for hobbyists.

RUNNING PLIERS These pliers are designed to apply equal pressure on both sides of the score line forcing the score to "run" or break along its length. They are used mainly for breaking score lines that are long and straight or gently curved. With practice, they can be used to start breaks on more difficult score lines. Running pliers are manufactured from metal or plastic. Metal running pliers have a concave jaw (placed on top side of glass) and a convex jaw (placed on underside of glass) that allows the breaking of narrow pieces of glass. They also have the strength to carry a "run" over a longer distance. Plastic running pliers have 3 teeth–2 on the top jaw and one on the lower jaw. These pliers are limited in how narrow a piece they can break since all 3 teeth need to be in contact with the glass. The plastic handles allow a fair amount of flex which reduces the length of the "run" these pliers can create. Some pliers have a central guide mark on the top jaw to assist in aligning the pliers on top of the glass correctly.

LEAD KNIPPERS Sometimes referred to as lead dykes, this tool is designed specifically for cutting and mitering lead came. Its jaws are ground flat on one side to produce a clean cut on the lead came.

SIDECUTTERS This tool has pointed jaws and produces only pointed cuts. Sidecutters will cut lengths of zinc came, but are not suitable for lead came.

LATHEKIN This tool's main uses are for burnishing copper foil and for widening the channel in various metal cames. The lathekin is sometimes referred to as a "fid."

GLASS GRINDER Complex and detailed shapes, and more sophisticated and creative designs are now possible with the aid of a glass grinder with diamond coated bits. Rough and uneven edges of cut pieces of glass can be smoothed and ground to fit a pattern more accurately. Excess glass on tight inside curves can be ground away, reducing the risk of cracking a piece during the breaking or grozing process.

Grinders allow the craftsperson to create

stained glass projects from smaller and more intricate pieces of glass. A ground edge on individual glass pieces also aids in the adhesion of the copper foil to the glass. A reservoir containing water traps the dust produced when grinding and helps prevent hazardous airborne glass particles. A face shield and back splash are recommended to contain any larger glass chips or overspray of water that may occur during the grinding process. For most hobbyists one of the mid-size reasonably priced grinders is sufficient to complete any project.

DRILLING/GRINDING BIT Many models of glass grinders come with a drilling/grinding bit (usually 1/4 in) to grind tight inside curves and drill holes. The position of the drilling bit on the grinder shaft is raised up from the grinder surface and will not come in contact with the moistened sponge. Since it needs to be wet, moisten the bit often with water or a mixture of water and grinding coolant.

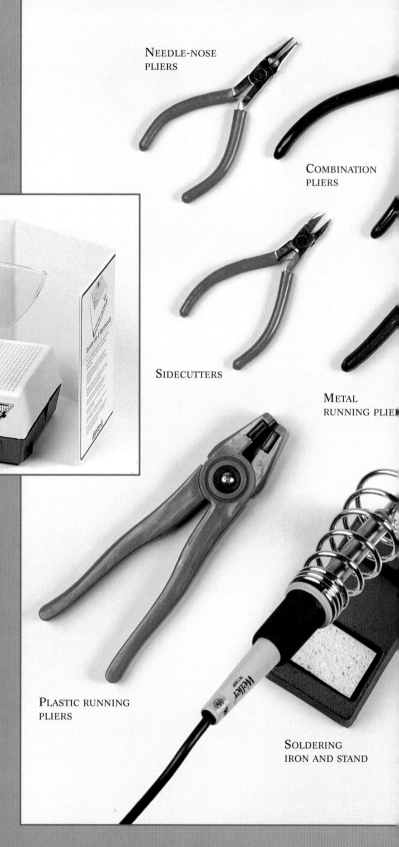

SOLDERING IRON AND STAND This tool melts the tin-lead alloy solder that joins pieces of copper foiled glass together. The iron must have a chisel-shaped tip to ensure a smooth and even solder seam and should be between 80 and 150 watts (a 100-watt iron is the most commonly used by hobbyists). For ease of soldering, the iron must be able to maintain a constant and even temperature (600 to 900°F). Many models have a built-in temperature control. Tips are available in a variety of widths and can be changed to accommodate the type of soldering being done. A stand is required to hold the soldering iron while it is hot and a sponge made of natural fibers is necessary to clean the tip during the soldering process.

LEAD VISE This tool is used to stretch lengths of lead came to straighten and remove kinks and to make the came more rigid. The vise, attached to the surface of a worktable, is used as a clamp on one end of the came while the lead is being pulled from the other end with a pair of pliers.

NEEDLE-NOSE PLIERS

COMBINATION PLIERS

SIDECUTTERS

METAL RUNNING PLIERS

PLASTIC RUNNING PLIERS

SOLDERING IRON AND STAND

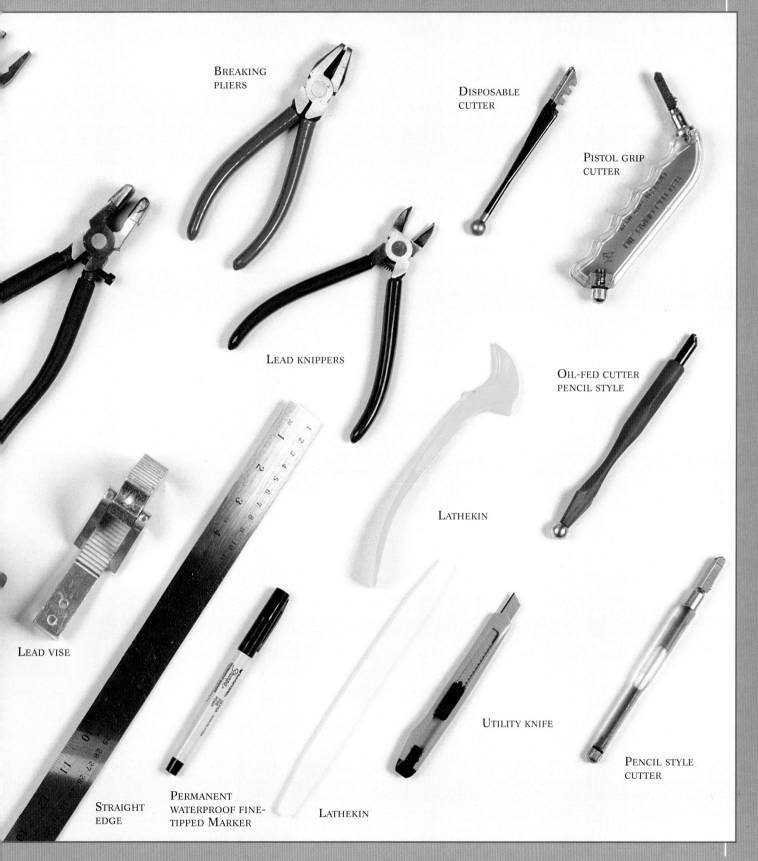

BREAKING
PLIERS

DISPOSABLE
CUTTER

PISTOL GRIP
CUTTER

LEAD KNIPPERS

OIL-FED CUTTER
PENCIL STYLE

LATHEKIN

LEAD VISE

STRAIGHT
EDGE

PERMANENT
WATERPROOF FINE-
TIPPED MARKER

LATHEKIN

UTILITY KNIFE

PENCIL STYLE
CUTTER

The Work Area

Choose a comfortable working space with enough room to spread out the project. A working area requires:
• a large, sturdy table or workbench with a smooth, level work surface (preferably plywood). The table should be at comfortable working height (around waist level).
• good overhead lighting (natural light if possible).
• an electrical outlet with grounded circuit for soldering irons and glass grinders.
• an easy-to-clean hard surfaced floor.
• a rack or wooden bin with dividers to store sheets of glass in an upright position. Store smaller pieces in a cardboard box.
• good ventilation (window, fan) when soldering or working with patinas.
• a supply of newspaper to cover work surface for easy cleaning.
• access to water to clean project and operate glass grinder.
• light table for tracing patterns onto hard-to-see-through glass. All that is required is a plywood box with a fluorescent fixture placed inside and 1/4 in clear float glass for the top. The underside of the glass must be sandblasted to diffuse the light from the bulbs. (Most shops selling float glass will be able to do this for you.)

When tracing patterns onto smaller pieces of glass, the following method can be used in place of a light table: tape the pattern onto an outside facing window, place the glass on top of the pattern, and trace your pattern onto the glass. This method is not recommended for large pieces of glass.

Make Your Own Light Table

Construct a plywood box 43 in x 25 in x 5-1/4 in. Place a fluorescent light fixture inside. Make a hole in one end for the light cord. Buy a piece of clear float glass 42 in x 24 in x 1/4 in thick. The

Safety Practices

Following these common sense rules will ensure a safe and healthy work environment. We do not recommend that young children work with stained glass. Pregnant women are advised to check with their physician.

1 Always wear safety glasses to prevent the risk of injury to eyes from small glass fragments that may become airborne during cutting and grinding, and splatters of flux and solder.

2 Do not eat, drink, or smoke while working with stained glass because over-exposure to lead may occur from ingesting it orally. This can happen if food, drink, or cigarettes are placed on a lead-tainted surface or handled with hands that have come in contact with lead (primarily during the soldering stage). Keep hands away from mouth and face and wash hands, arms, and face thoroughly with soap and water.

3 Cover all cuts and scrapes with an adhesive plaster when working with lead or solder. Lead cannot be absorbed through the skin but can enter through open sores and cuts.

4 Wear a work apron to protect clothing as well as help prevent the spread of glass fragments and lead particles around your home. Wash work apron separately from other clothes.

5 Wear closed shoes to prevent glass fragments from coming in contact with your feet.

6 Clean your work area and floor surface with a damp mop or wet sponge. Sweeping or vacuuming may cause minute lead particles to become airborne and be inhaled by anyone in the immediate area.

NOTE   Because lead fumes are produced in such minute quantities at the temperatures required for stained glass soldering, there is little danger of lead inhalation. However, there can be some mist produced as the flux is burned off during soldering. Though the mist produced by safety flux is generally considered harmless, it is a good idea to work in a well ventilated area and, if possible, with a small fan to pull the mist away from you. If ventilation is a concern, wear a respirator with filters designed to screen out mists and vapors. For pertinent information on respirators, visit your local safety supply store.

7 Carry glass in a vertical position with one hand supporting the sheet from below and the other hand steadying the sheet from the side. Wear gloves when moving larger sheets.

shop selling the glass will often sandblast it on one side to diffuse the light from the bulbs. To trace patterns, place pattern on the light table, and position the art glass on top of the pattern. Trace the pattern outline.

Basic Techniques

How to Select Glass for the Project

The combination of color, texture, and light determines how the finished piece will look. Selecting glass is an exciting part of the craft but for the novice it may be intimidating. Here are some guidelines:

1 View the glass to be selected in lighting conditions similar to those where your finished project will be displayed. For pieces that will not be transmitting light, select glasses that are lighter in color and attractive in reflective light.

2 Try to keep color selections to a minimum. The larger a project is in size, the more color variations that can be introduced. In small projects, focus on 2 or 3 colors. If a wider range of glass is needed, try using clear textured glasses or varying shades of one of the dominant colors. View glass choices side by side to see how the colors affect each other. Bold colors may need to be softened by surrounding them with lighter colors and clear textured glasses.

3 Opalescent glass is often used for the main body of a lamp shade to disguise the electrical components and to soften the effect of the light bulb.

4 On pp 44, 64 and 84 we have shown other glass and color choices for patterns. There are many possibilities and this is part of the pleasure of creating stained glass.

NOTE *Amounts of glass listed for individual projects are exact for that pattern. You may wish to purchase more glass to allow for matching glass textures and grain or for possible breakage. Take the pattern with you when purchasing glass from a stained glass retailer.*

How to Copy the Patterns

Since you will need 2 or 3 copies of the pattern for each project, be sure all pattern copies are accurate.

PHOTOCOPYING This is the easiest method for making duplicate copies. Be sure to verify each copy with the original pattern, especially for 3-dimensional projects such as lamp shades, boxes, and vases. Some projects use precut bevels and jewels so it is also important that they fit the pattern. Many photocopiers can also enlarge or reduce patterns.

NOTE When enlarging patterns, the space between glass pieces should remain at 1/32 in.

TRACING Lay tracing vellum over the pattern and trace the lines of the design. Only one copy can be made at a time. But you can make several copies at once using carbon sheets. Lay a sheet of paper on the work surface and place a carbon face down overtop. For each copy you require, add another layer of paper and carbon. Place the project pattern on top and fasten in place, using push pins or tape. Trace the outline of the pattern, pressing firmly so that the image is transferred through to each layer of paper.

GRID METHOD Grid work can be used to enlarge, reduce, or change the dimensions of a design. On paper large enough to accommodate the desired size, draw a new grid work with the size of squares adjusted to fit the new grid. Copy the design from the original grid onto the modified one, square by square. NOTE *For sizing reference, patterns in this book that are not full size are placed on grid work–1 square = 1 in.*

BLUEPRINTING By tracing the project pattern onto drawing vellum, exact copies can be made by a blueprinting firm. Blueprints are exact and do not distort the pattern in any way.

OVERHEAD AND OPAQUE PROJECTORS Projectors can be used to enlarge pattern designs, but patterns will be distorted and will require adjustments. We recommend using this method as a guideline only. When enlarging patterns with bevels or other pieces that must be a certain size, the pattern will have to be altered accordingly.

NOTE When enlarging patterns, the space between glass pieces should remain at 1/32 in.

Transferring the Pattern Onto the Glass

For accurate glass cutting it is advisable to draw the outline of the piece to be cut directly onto the glass. Try to position the pattern piece on the glass sheet to avoid excessive waste when cutting. And take into account the pattern or texture of the glass piece you are cutting and how it will flow with the other glass pieces around it. Leave approximately 1/4 in around the piece so the breaking pliers will have something to grasp when breaking the score line.

For many translucent and light-colored opalescent glasses, the pattern can be transferred by simply placing the sheet of glass directly on the pattern copy and tracing the design lines with a permanent waterproof fine-tipped marker. A light box will help illuminate the pattern from below, but it is not essential. For opaque glass, the pattern can be transferred by making a template of the pieces to be cut (using the tracing method described on p16) and tracing around the template perimeter, onto the glass. Use cardstock or lightweight cardboard for making the template. An alternative method is to place a carbon sheet face down on the glass with the pattern on top. By pressing firmly on the lines with a pen or pencil, the pattern will be transferred onto the glass. Go over the carbon lines with the marker.

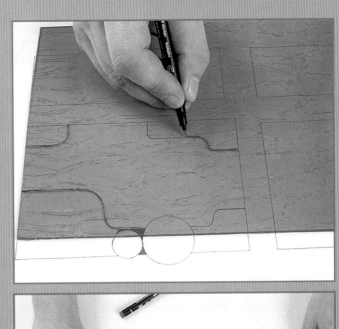

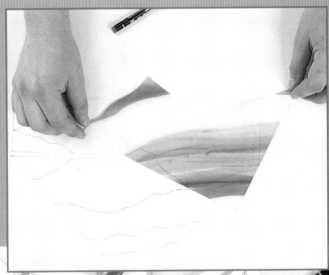

How to Make a Jig

To make a jig, tape a copy of the pattern to a wood board (slightly larger than the project) and nail pieces of wood trim along the perimeter of the pattern. This will keep the project's shape true to the pattern during the soldering stage.

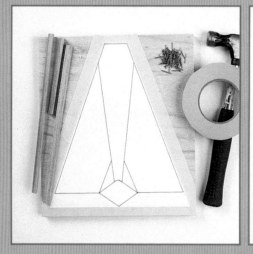
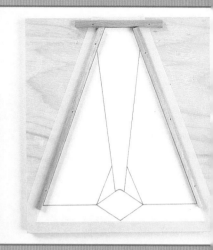

How to Cut Glass—The Basics

Cutting (scoring and breaking) glass properly is a learned technique.
Use 3mm float glass (windowpane glass) to practise cutting flow and amount of pressure to exert. Draw patterns A, B, C, D, E, and F (pp19–21) on windowpane glass and practise the techniques of scoring and breaking before starting a project.

1 Wear safety glasses and a work apron. Stand in an upright position before the worktable.

2 Work on a clean, level, non-skid work surface covered with newspaper.

3 Place the glass smooth side up, on which the pattern has been traced with the marker.

4 Hold the cutter in your writing hand perpendicular to the glass, not tilted to the left or the right. Run the cutter away from your body and inside the pattern lines, applying steady pressure as you score.

See photographs below for different styles of cutters. Carbide steel wheel cutters will last for many years as opposed to disposable cutters.

5 Start and finish at an edge of the glass. Do not stop or lift your cutter from the glass surface before the score is completed. Use a fluid motion, applying constant, even pressure.

6 Never go over a score line a second time.

7 Grasp the glass with a hand on each side of the score line, thumbs parallel to the score, knuckles touching. Roll wrists up and outward, breaking the glass along the scored line.

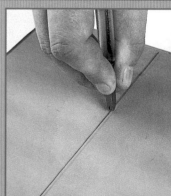

Left: Disposable cutter held in traditional manner. The cutter rests between the index and middle fingers with the ball of the thumb placed to push the cutter along. The wheel must be lubricated before each score and wears out quickly.

Second: Oil-fed cutter held in traditional manner. If wheel and housing wear, they can be replaced.

Third: Pistol grip cutter held in palm of hand with the thumb resting on top of the barrel and index finger guiding cutter head.

Fourth: Pencil-style cutter, oil-fed, and held as a pencil.

To increase the probability of a good score and prolong the life of the glass cutter:
• Make sure the surface of the glass is clean and free of any debris.
• Score on the smoothest side of the glass.
• Lubricate the wheel of the glass cutter before each score. If a self-oiling cutter is being used, it will oil itself—but check occasionally to ensure that there is oil in the reservoir. Wipe away any small glass fragments that may have collected on the cutter wheel.
• Keep the cutter wheel covered when not in use.

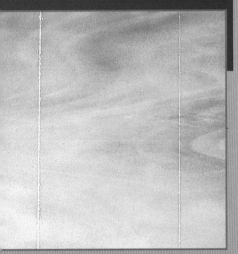

In the above photo—left: score line with too much pressure; right: score line with correct pressure

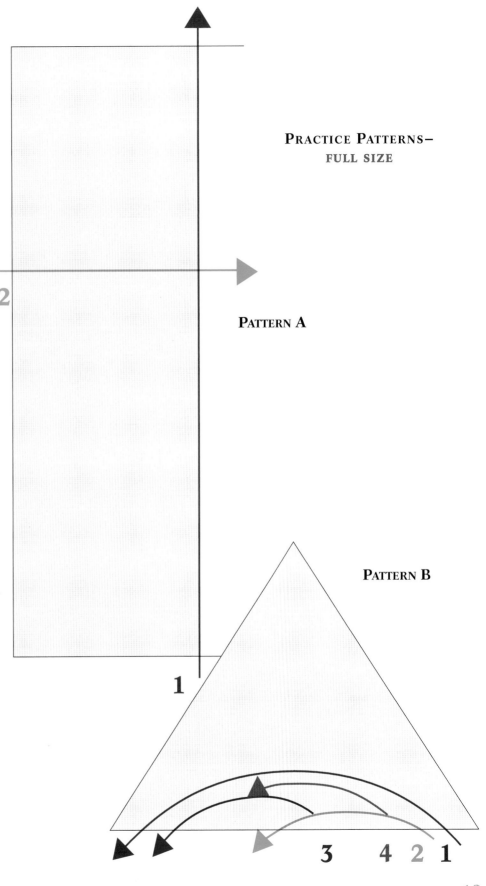

PRACTICE PATTERNS—
FULL SIZE

PATTERN A

PATTERN B

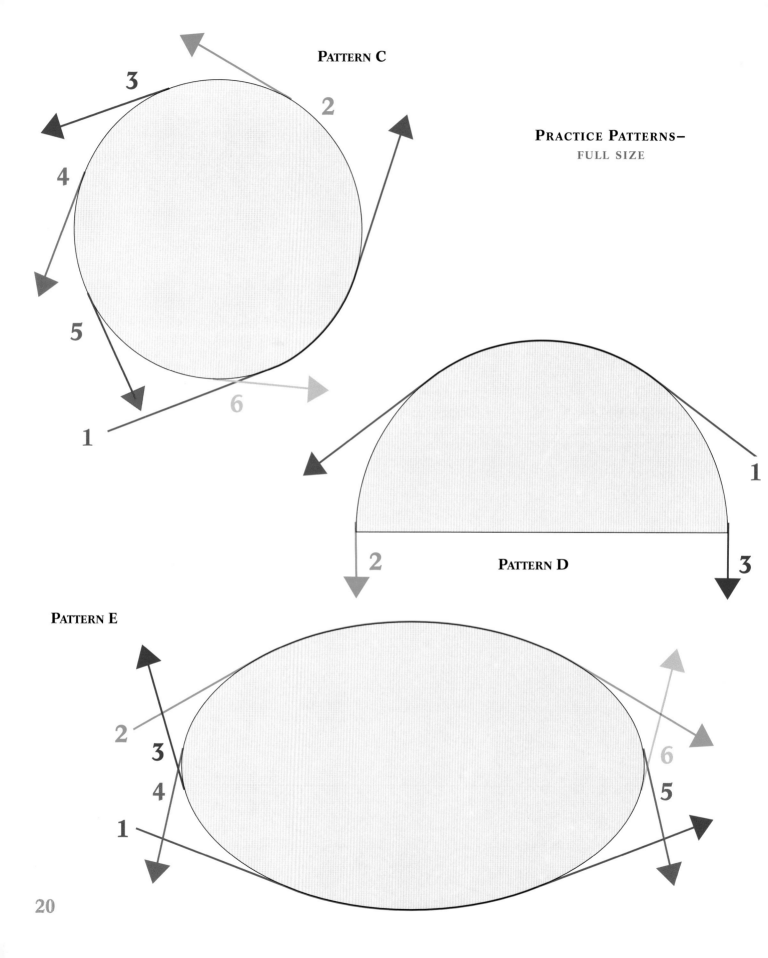

PATTERN C

PRACTICE PATTERNS–
FULL SIZE

PATTERN D

PATTERN E

20

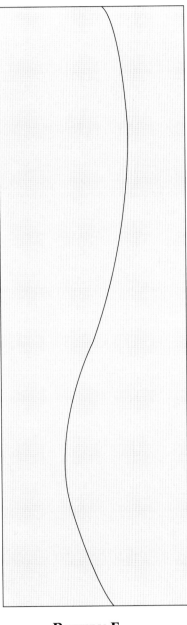

PATTERN F

How to Break Glass on a Score Line

Glass can also be broken using running pliers. This works for breaking straight lines and slight curves and is also useful for starting a break at either end of a score line. If you use metal running pliers, the slightly concave jaw must be placed on the topside of the glass and the convex jaw on the underside. If you use plastic running pliers, position the jaw with the 2 outside "teeth" or ridges on the top side of the glass.

USING RUNNING PLIERS

1 Position the running pliers so that the score line is centered and the glass is partially inside the jaws, approximately 1/2 in to 3/4 in.

2 Gently squeeze the handles and the score will "run" (travel), causing the glass to break off into 2 pieces. If the "run" does not go the full length of the score line, repeat the procedure at the other end of the score line.

USING BREAKING PLIERS OR COMBINATION PLIERS

Breaking pliers have 2 identical flat, smooth jaws that can be placed on either side of the glass. Combination pliers have a flat top jaw and a curved bottom jaw—both are serrated.

1 Position the pliers perpendicular to the score line and as close as possible without touching it. Start at either end of the score line (not the middle).

2 Use an out-and-downward pulling motion on the pliers to break the glass.

3 When using 2 sets of pliers to break apart 2 smaller pieces of glass, place the pliers on the glass on either side of the score line and opposite to each other. Hold one set of pliers steady and use an out-and-downward pulling motion with the other set to separate the glass piece.

Using running pliers

Using breaking or combination pliers

21

A Useful Technique for Making a Straight Cut

SCORING WITH CORKED-BACK STRAIGHTEDGE

1 Mark the line to be cut and position the straightedge parallel and approximately 1/8 in from the line.
2 Holding the straightedge firmly on the surface of the glass, make the score line by pulling the cutter toward your body.
3 Break the score line, using the method you feel most comfortable with (pp18 and 21).

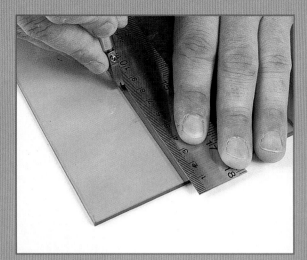

A Last-Resort-Technique for Difficult-to-Break Glass Pieces

TAPPING UNDERNEATH A SCORE LINE

NOTE   Tapping a score line may cause small chips and fractures along the score line and should be done only as a last resort on difficult-to-break pieces. Here's how to do it.
1 Hold the glass close to the surface of the worktable. Using the ball at the end of the cutter, gently strike the glass from the underside, directly underneath the score line. Once the score begins to "run," continue tapping ahead of the "run" until it reaches the other end of the score line.
2 With your hands or a pair of pliers, separate the glass into 2 pieces.

Breaking Larger Sheets of Art Glass

1 Score the sheet of glass, using a straightedge as a guide for the cutter.
2 Align the score line with the edge of the worktable.
3 Grasping the glass firmly and using both hands, raise the end of the sheet, approximately 1 in from the surface of the table. The opposite end of the sheet must still be in contact with the table.
4 With a swift, downward motion, snap off the end piece of glass.

Cutting Squares and Rectangles

Because it is almost impossible to cut glass at a 90° angle, a series of straight scores and breaks is recommended when cutting square and rectangular pieces.

1 Trace pattern A (p19) onto the glass, aligning one of the sides of the pattern with the edge of the glass.

2 Score along the other side of the pattern piece. Proceed to break the score line, using any method described previously.

3 Score and break any remaining cut required to achieve the shape of the pattern piece.

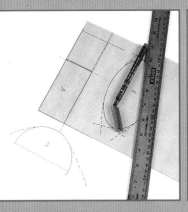 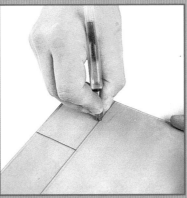 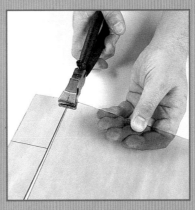 

Cutting Inside Curves

Inside curves are the most difficult cuts to score and break out successfully. Attempt the most difficult cut of a piece first, before cutting the piece away from the large sheet of glass.

1 Trace pattern B (p19) onto the glass. Position the outer edges of the curve so they align with the edge of the glass.

2 Score the inside curve of the pattern piece but do not attempt to break it out at this time.

3 Make several smaller concave score lines (scallops) between the initial score line and the outside edge of the glass.

4 Using breaker or combination pliers, start removing the scallops, one at a time, beginning with the one closest to the edge of the glass. Use a pulling action with the pliers rather than a downward motion. Remember to position the jaws of the pliers at either end of the score line and not in the middle.

5 Continue to break away the scallops until you reach the initial score line. Remove it and proceed to score and break away the pattern piece from the large piece.

NOTE   The tapping method of running a score line can be used, with care, to break out stubborn pieces.

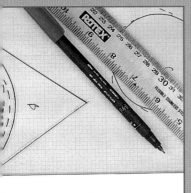 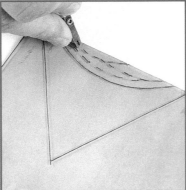  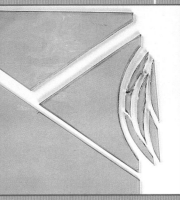

Cutting Outside Curves, Circles, and Ovals

1 Trace pattern C (p20) onto the glass, leaving 1/2 in from the outside edge of the glass.

2 Make an initial score line that will separate the pattern piece from the sheet of glass. The score line will go from the outside edge of the glass and upon reaching the circle will follow the perimeter of it for a short distance and then head off on a tangent to the edge of the glass (*see* line 1). Break away this piece.

3 The second score line will follow around the circle for a short distance (approximately 1/6th of the perimeter) and then leave on a tangent to the outside edge (*see* line 2).
Break away this piece.

4 Repeat step 3, scoring and breaking the glass in a pinwheel fashion, until the circle shape has been formed (*see* lines 3, 4, 5, and 6).

5 Small jagged edges where a score line was started or ended can be ground off with a glass grinder or nibbled away with breaking or combination pliers (*see* Grozing, p25).

6 To practise cutting outside curves and ovals, trace pattern D and E (p20) onto the glass, leaving 1/2 in from the outside edge of the glass. Follow steps 2 to 5 above.

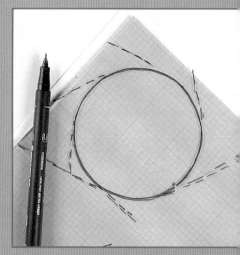

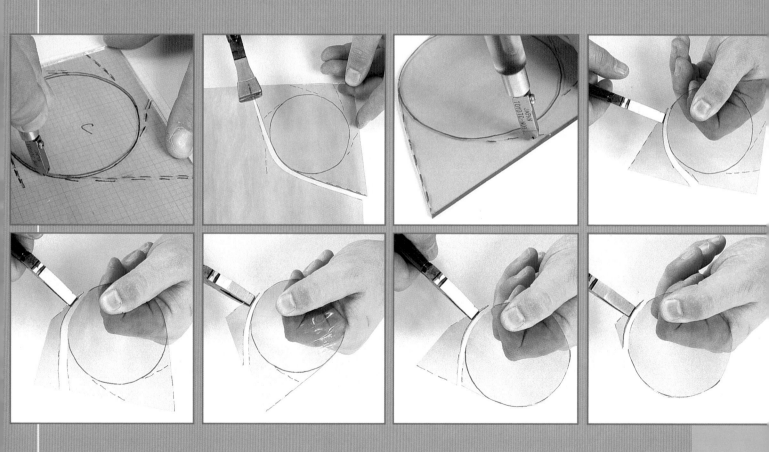

Scoring and Breaking S-Shaped Curves

1 Trace pattern F (p21) onto the glass, placing one of the sides against the edge of the glass.
2 Score the most difficult cut first (S-shape).
3 Align the running pliers with the score line. Squeeze only hard enough to start the run. Repeat the procedure at the opposite end of the score line. If both runs meet, use your hands to separate the resulting 2 pieces. If the "runs" do not meet, gently tap along the the score line (on the underside of the glass).
4 Score and break out remaining cuts.

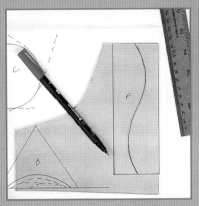

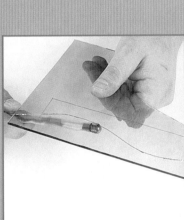

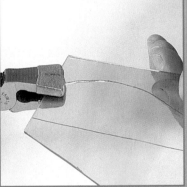

Grozing

The jagged edge of the glass along the score line can be smoothed by grozing.
1 Grasping the piece of glass firmly in one hand, place the combination pliers perpendicular to the edge of the glass and drag the serrated jaws along the jagged edge in an up-and-down motion. Repeat until the edge of the glass is smooth.

25

How to Grind Glass

1 Wear safety glasses and a work apron, have a face shield attached to the grinder, and position a back splash along the back and sides of the grinder to contain any airborne glass chips and water overspray.

2 Keep water in the reservoir and have a moistened sponge positioned adjacent to the diamond-coated bit at all times.

3 Cut each glass piece on the inside of the pattern line to fit the pattern with less grinding and allow for the application of copper foil. If the glass pieces fit the pattern and do not overlap the pattern line, make one quick swipe against the grinding bit on each edge of the glass to dull any sharp edges. Only light pressure is required when pushing the glass against the bit.

4 If traces of the marked line are still visible on the piece, grind the edge to ensure an accurate fit within the pattern lines.

5 Check the piece again with the pattern. If any part of the piece still overlaps, mark the area with a permanent waterproof marker. Grind the excess away. Check the piece with the pattern. Repeat until the piece fits.

6 Repeat steps 3 through 5 for each piece, making sure to leave a very narrow space between the pieces to accommodate the copper foil. Pieces that leave a large gap between the line and the adjacent piece should be recut.

7 Rinse each glass piece under clear running water when grinding is complete.

8 Wipe the surface of the grinder often with a wet sponge or cloth to prevent small glass chips from scratching the underside of the pieces being ground. Do not run bare hands across the grid work. Glass slivers are painful and difficult to remove.

9 To ensure proper performance of the glass grinder, clean thoroughly and rinse the water reservoir after each use.

NOTE   Keep the pattern sheet dry during the grinding stage by placing it inside a vinyl sheet protector or cover it with an adhesive-backed clear vinyl.

How to Grind Inside Curves Using a Drilling/Grinding Bit

1 Wear safety glasses and a work apron. Grasp the glass piece firmly in your writing hand and grind away excess glass by holding it against the bit with a light and even pressure. In the other hand, hold a moistened piece of sponge lightly against the bit to keep it wet.
2 Check the piece against the project pattern and mark where further grinding is required. Repeat until the piece fits accurately.

NOTE   An elevated platform, used as a surface on which to rest small glass pieces when using drilling bits for grinding, is available for most makes and models of grinders.

How to Drill a Hole

1 With a permanent waterproof fine-tipped marker, mark the glass piece where the hole is to be drilled. Holding the glass at an angle to the top of the bit, begin grinding the hole. Hold the glass firmly but do not apply too much pressure.
2 Once the hole has been started, level out the glass piece and continue to grind completely through the glass. Wet the bit often with a sponge soaked with water and/or grinding coolant.

NOTE   If the glass is opaque and you cannot see where to grind the hole, make a template of the glass piece from stiff cardboard. Make a hole large enough for the drilling bit to fit through. Tape the template to the underside of the glass. With the template facing downward, drill the glass, using the hole in the template as your guide. To preserve the template for later use, remove it from the glass once the hole has been started.

How to Prepare Mirrored Glass

1 Always cut mirrored glass on the glass side, not the silvered side.
2 Bevel the coated side of the mirror by holding it at a 45° angle to the grinder work surface, with the silver-backing facing up, and lightly grind each edge. Beveling will help prevent chipping the silvering during grinding.
3 Grind mirror, if required, to make it fit the pattern. Keep the grinding surface clean to prevent scratching the silvering.
4 Rinse off grinding residue with clean water and dry with a soft cloth.
5 Apply clear nail polish to the edges of the mirror to prevent flux or patina from seeping between the glass and the silvering. Allow polish to dry.
6 Apply the appropriate copper foil (p29) to the edges.

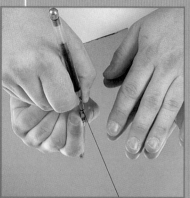   

How to Prepare Beveled Glass

1 Beveled glass that is precut can be purchased from your local glass dealer.
Verify that the bevels fit the pattern and grind (p26) to fit if they do not.
2 Take care not to scratch the glass bevels. Keep work surfaces clean. Place masking tape over the raised surface of the bevels for protection from scratches.
3 Apply the appropriate copper foil (p29) to the edges.

NOTE   This procedure also applies to purchased jewels, glass globs or nuggets, and rondels.

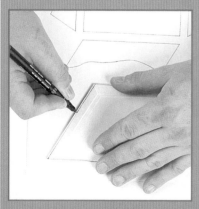  

How to Apply Copper Foil

1 All pieces of glass must be clean and dry before being wrapped in copper foil or the adhesive backing will not stick to the edge of the glass.
2 Choose the backing and width of foil best suited for the project. Use regular foil (copper-backed foil) if seams are to be treated with copper patina, black-backed foil for black seams, and silver-backed foil for silver seams.

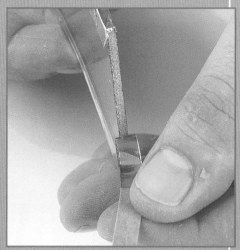

NOTE   We often use black-backed foil regardless of the color of the seams because it gives the appearance of a shadow and is quite unnoticeable.

Copper foil is available in various widths—1/8 in to 12 in—the most commonly used are 3/16 in, 7/32 in, and 1/4 in. For most projects in this book, 7/32 in foil is required. When a single piece of glass varies greatly in thickness, use a wider foil and trim it evenly with a utility knife.

3 Peel 2 in to 3 in of the paper backing away from the foil and lightly grasp the foil between your thumb and index finger. The adhesive-covered side should be facing upward. With your writing hand, center the edge of the glass on the foil, leaving an equal amount of foil showing on either side of the piece. Fold the edges of the foil over and press firmly to the glass. Foiling should be started at a corner of the piece that will be positioned towards the center of the project.
4 Hold the glass piece in your writing hand, perpendicular to the work surface. *See* photographs. Press the foil onto the glass by sliding the middle and ring fingers of your opposite hand along the edge. Let the foil slide through the thumb and index finger, automatically peeling the backing off the foil. You should have a clear view of both sides of the glass as the foil is being applied. Continue wrapping the foil around the entire piece, making sure to keep it centered.

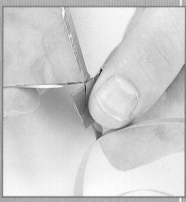

5 Once the entire piece has been wrapped, cut the foil with a utility knife or scissors, overlapping the starting edge approximately 1/4 in. *Crimp* (fold and press) the edges of the foil onto the surface of the glass, using a lathekin or a piece of wooden doweling.
6 *Burnish* (press and rub) the foil firmly to the glass along the perimeter of the piece and the edges of the foil. This will ensure proper adhesion to the glass when heat is applied to the copper foil during the soldering stage.

NOTE   Orange peelers, pencils and pens, popsicle sticks, can be used successfully to burnish foil.
7 Trim excess or overlap with a utility knife.

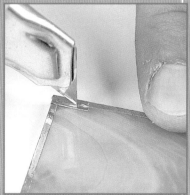

How to Solder

1   Choose a well ventilated area and a level work surface. Wear safety glasses and a work apron.

2   Plug in soldering iron (we recommend 100-watt style with built-in temperature control, chisel-style tip, and stand).

3   To wipe the tip clean while soldering, moisten a natural fiber sponge with water and place in the holder on the soldering iron stand.

4   Lay out 60/40 solder and a safety flux.

5   While the soldering iron is heating up, assemble the copper foiled pieces on the project pattern.

6   *Tack solder* the pieces together by dabbing flux (using a cotton swab) onto the copper foil at a point where at least 2 pieces meet. Then unwind several inches of the solder wire from the spool. Grasp the soldering iron handle like a hammer, in your writing hand, and remove from the stand. Melt a small amount of solder onto the tip of the iron and apply it to the fluxed copper foil. Hold the iron tip on the copper foil only long enough for the solder to melt onto the foil, joining the pieces together.

7   Working your way around the project, flux and tack solder all the pieces together, making sure to tack wherever 2 or more pieces join. If a piece is tacked in several spots, it will not move out of position when the finishing seam is being soldered. At regular intervals, wipe the tip of the soldering iron on the moistened sponge to remove flux residue.

8   *Tinning*—Once all the pieces have been tacked together, the exposed copper foil must be coated with a thin, flat layer of solder. First apply flux along the entire length of a foiled seam. Then holding the soldering iron in your writing hand, place the flat side of the iron tip on the fluxed copper foil and, grasping the spool of solder in the other hand, place the end of the solder on the tip. As the solder melts, pull the tip along the seam, leaving a thin coating of solder over the foil. Fill in any gaps between the stained glass pieces with solder.

9   *Bead soldering* gives seams a rounded and even finish. To do this reapply flux along one seam. Place the narrower side of the iron tip onto one end of the seam (the flat side will now be in a vertical position), keeping the tip in contact with the seam at all times. Holding the solder to the tip, slowly draw the iron along the length of the seam allowing

30

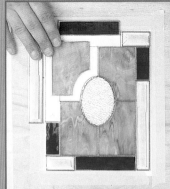
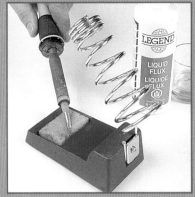
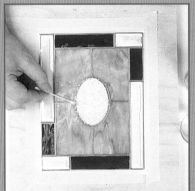

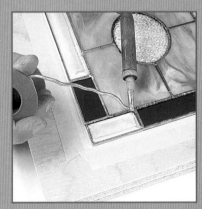

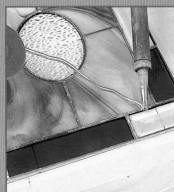

the solder to build up only enough to create a slightly raised, half-round seam. When the solder begins to build up more than necessary, pull the strand of solder away from the tip. Draw the tip along the seam until the molten solder levels out more evenly. It will take a bit of practise to determine how quickly to move the iron and how much solder to apply. Because glass can crack if it is heated too much, don't go over a solder seam too many times. Allow the area to cool while you solder another seam. Flux and bead solder the remaining seams.

10   Turn the project over and tin and bead solder each seam on the reverse side, as described in the steps above.

11   To finish the outside edges of a project that will not be utilizing a rigid metal border (zinc or lead came), flux and tin all exposed copper foil on both sides. Holding the project in a vertical position, bead the edge by applying a small amount of solder and

 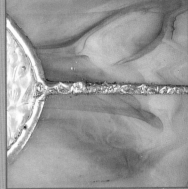

then lifting the iron off the foil long enough for it to cool before adding more. Use a touch-and-lift motion rather than drawing the iron along the edge. This will prevent the copper foil from becoming too hot and lifting off the edges of the glass. Repeat around the outside perimeter of the project. (Other methods of finishing the outside edges will be demonstrated in various projects throughout the book.)

12   Remove excess flux residue quickly to eliminate oxidization and a tarnished look (*see* Cleaning the Project, p33).

Common Soldering Problems

Soldering can be a difficult technique to master. Here are some problems and tips to correct them.

1   THE MOLTEN SOLDER IS NOT BONDING TO THE COPPER FOIL—Apply flux and try again. If you have already been soldering on this seam and had applied flux, it probably has evaporated. If your glass pieces were foiled some time ago, the copper foil may have a layer of oxidization on it. To remove oxidization, gently rub fine steel wool (000) lengthwise along the foil. Apply flux and try soldering again.

2   SOLDER MELTS THROUGH SEAMS—The soldering tip has probably been held too long in one place. Solder in another area of the project until the seam cools and try again.

3   MELT-THROUGH IS OCCURRING BECAUSE OF LARGE GAPS BETWEEN PIECES—Cutting glass pieces accurately to fit the pattern will prevent many soldering problems. Large gaps between pieces can be responsible for melt-throughs, especially in 3-dimensional projects. By tinning 3-D projects with 50/50 solder and then bead soldering with 60/40 solder, solder will not melt

 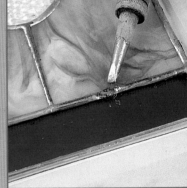

through as quickly. Placing masking tape on the underside of the gap will help hold the molten solder in place long enough for it to cool.

4 COPPER FOIL IS LIFTING FROM THE GLASS DURING SOLDERING STAGE—The copper foil may have been overheated during the soldering stage. To prevent the foil from lifting
• make sure the glass is free of oil and grinding residue before applying copper foil;
• start and end the foil on the glass piece on an edge that will not be on the perimeter of a project; the point where the foil overlaps should be on an inside seam;
• burnish the foil tightly to the glass;
• do not draw the soldering iron over a seam time after time without letting the seam cool occasionally;
• be sure adhesive backing on the copper foil has not dried out and lost its stickiness.

5 SOLDER SEAMS HAVE PEAKS AND VALLEYS— Reapply flux and touch up the seam with your soldering iron. Hold the tip to the solder long enough to start melting it and then lift the tip up and repeat the melt-and-lift motion along the seam, smoothing it out. Add solder, if required.

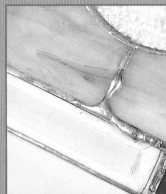

6 TOO MUCH SOLDER ON A SEAM—Excess solder can be removed by melting the solder and quickly dragging the iron tip across the seam, taking excess solder with it. Immediately remove the excess solder from the iron tip by wiping it on a moistened sponge.

7 SOLDER IS SPATTERING AND CREATING SMALL PITS IN THE SOLDER SEAM—You may be using too much flux. Use a safety flux formulated for stained glass work and use it sparingly.

8 SOLDER IS NOT FLOWING PROPERLY, RESULTING IN UNEVEN SOLDER SEAMS—
To prevent this
• The tip of the iron may be dirty. Clean iron tip on a natural fiber sponge moistened with water or if spots develop that will not disappear when tip is wiped on the sponge, retin the tip.
• The tip is not hot enough or the tip is too hot causing the solder to melt through the seams. On irons that have adjustable temperature controls, try different settings until you find the one that works best for you.
• Flux needs to be reapplied.

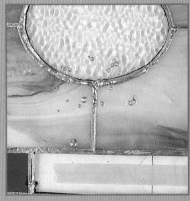

Cleaning the Project

Once the project has been soldered together, clean thoroughly to remove any flux residue. If not removed quickly, flux solutions, because of their corrosive nature, will cause the solder seams to oxidize resulting in a tarnished look. To clean, apply a small amount of cleaning solution to your project. With a soft cloth or an old toothbrush moistened with warm water, rub the cleaner over the entire project. Rinse under warm running water until all traces of flux and cleaner are removed. Do not immerse project in water. Dry with a soft cloth. Commercial stained glass cleaning solutions are referred to as neutralizing solutions. They are formulated to counteract the effects of flux as they clean. Household liquid dish detergent can also be used effectively when mixed with a small amount of sodium bicarbonate.

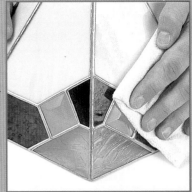

HOW TO FINISH THE PROJECT

Solder seams can be finished in a number of ways—left as they are (shiny silver) or lightly rubbed with steel wool for a pewter look, or color altered by applying a black or copper patina. Apply patina after the project has been soldered and cleaned for best results.

Applying Patina

1   Cover the work surface with a layer of newspaper. Wear rubber gloves and a work apron to protect your hands and clothing from the patina. Wear safety glasses.

2   If the project sits overnight or you have decided at a later date to apply patina, remove the oxidization on the metal's surface by rubbing fine steel wool (000) across all solder seams. By rubbing across, not lengthwise, any cooling lines in the solder will become less visible and give the appearance of a smoother line.

3   Use a soft cloth to brush off any traces of steel wool onto the newspaper. Roll the newspaper up and discard. Place a new layer of newspaper under the project.

4   Pour a small amount of patina out of the bottle into another container. This will prevent the risk of contaminating any unused patina. Apply the patina to the solder seams with an old toothbrush, cotton swabs, or soft disposable cloth and rub gently until you achieve an even finish. Try not to get patina on the glass. Because of metal oxides in stained glass, some glasses will incur a rainbow-like hazing where the patina touches the glass. Though it is not very noticeable, it is best to try and avoid it.

5   Clean the project thoroughly with warm water and a neutralizing solution and dry with a soft cloth.

6   If there is any patina left that was poured out of the original bottle, dispose of it. If a toothbrush was used, rinse it in clean water. Dispose of the newspaper and any cotton swabs or cloths used to apply the patina. Because the black or copper color is the result of a chemical reaction with the surface of the solder, the patina can be removed if you are not happy with the outcome by rubbing with fine steel wool (000).

7   Apply finishing compound or wax (p34)

Applying Finishing Compound or Wax

To keep solder seams bright and shiny and help prevent oxidization apply stained glass finishing compound or a quality car wax. Place a small portion of the liquid wax on a soft cloth and apply a thin layer over the solder seams. Avoid getting wax on heavily textured glass because it may be difficult to remove. Allow the wax to dry to a powdery consistency and buff the seams with a dry cloth until shiny. Use an old toothbrush along seams and crevices.

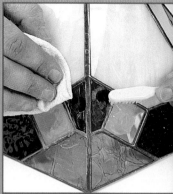

Maintaining the Finished Project

Clean the project with ammonia-free commercial window cleaner. If the seams have been treated with patina, they can be touched up if the patina wears off. Solder seams left the natural silver color can be rewaxed if they appear tarnished.

Diagonal Box and Lid, p96

34

How to Replace Cracked Pieces of Glass

Sooner or later, every stained glass artisan has to replace a cracked piece of glass. Here's how to do it:

1 Remove the broken piece using method A or B.

METHOD A a) Apply a hot soldering iron tip to the solder seams surrounding the broken piece. As the solder becomes molten, draw the iron tip across the solder seam, pulling the solder off the seam with the iron tip. Wipe excess solder off the tip onto the water-moistened sponge used for cleaning the tip. Repeat until the solder seam is flat.
b) Applying the hot iron tip to one of the seams, use a strip of aluminum (cut from a soda pop can) and try to wedge it between the broken piece and the one beside it, causing the solder to separate between the 2 pieces. Wrap the end of the aluminum strip that you hold with masking tape to prevent burns or cuts.
c) When you get the aluminum strip through the seam to the other side of the panel, pull it along the perimeter of the piece, heating the seams with the iron as you go.
d) When you have separated all the solder seams around the broken piece, it can be removed easily.

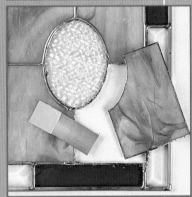

METHOD B a) With a glass cutter, make a number of scores on the broken piece in a crosshatch pattern.
b) Tap the scores gently on the underside with the end of the cutter, being careful not to crack the glass piece next to it.
c) Once the scores begin to "run" and break into small pieces, remove them with a pair of pliers.

2 When the broken glass piece has been removed, go around the entire opening with the soldering iron tip, smoothing away excess solder and pulling out any foil left behind from the broken piece with a pair of pliers.
3 Place a piece of paper beneath the opening and trace the outline of the empty space. Cut out this pattern inside the line.
4 Place the pattern on a new piece of glass and cut (pp18–25) with a glass cutter. Grind (p26) to fit and wrap with the appropriate copper foil (p29).
5 Position the replacement piece in the opening and tack solder (p30) into place. Proceed to bead solder (p30) on both sides of the project.
6 Apply patina (p33) to match the rest of the project, if required. Clean the project (p33) and apply a finishing compound or wax (p34).

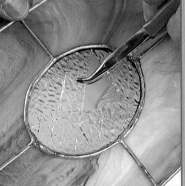

Small Hanging Panel

DIMENSIONS   7-1/4 in wide by 9-1/4 in high

NO. OF PIECES   13

GLASS REQUIRED

Letters refer to the type of glass used on pattern pieces (p39).

   A   5-1/2 in x 7-1/2 in lilac wispy
   B   3 in x 5 in grape cathedral
   C   3 in x 4 in clear textured
   D   2–1 in x 2 in clear rectangular bevels
   E   2–1 in x 6 in clear rectangular bevels

This quantity of glass is the exact amount needed for the pattern. You may have to purchase more glass. Please allow for matching textures and grain.

MATERIALS
2 copies of pattern
Newspaper
Wood board
Wood trim
Masking tape
Silver-backed copper foil
Safety flux
60/40 solder
1/8 in single channel
  U-shaped zinc came
18 to 20 gauge tinned
  copper wire
Neutralizing solution
Wax or finishing compound
Monofilament line (fishing
  line)

TOOLS
Apron
Safety glasses
Utility knife or scissors
Permanent waterproof fine-
tipped marker
Cork-backed straightedge
Glass cutter
Running pliers
Breaking pliers
Hammer and nails
Glass grinder
Soft cloths
Lathekin or doweling
Soldering iron and stand
Natural fiber sponge
Cotton swabs
Sidecutters or lead knippers
Small square
Toothbrush
Cup hook screws

Preparing the Pieces

1 Make 2 copies (p16) of the pattern on page 39. Use one copy as a guide for cutting and breaking the glass pieces. Use the second copy for fitting and soldering the panel together.

NOTE   If you use opalescent glass make a third copy and cut out the required pieces to use as a template.

2 Using the marker, trace (p17) each pattern piece on the glass to be cut.

3 Cut (pp18–25) each piece of glass required, making sure to cut *inside* the marker line. Use the cork-backed straightedge to assist in scoring straight lines (p22).

4 Make a jig (p18) to help fit the glass pieces together accurately.

5 Grind (p26) each piece of glass, as required, to fit the pattern. Remember to leave enough space between each piece so that the pattern line is visible between each piece (1/32 inch in width). After each piece is ground, rinse under clean water to remove any grinding residue and dry with a clean cloth.

6 Verify that the precut bevels fit the pattern and grind to fit where they do not (p28).

7 Choose the width of copper foil appropriate for the thickness of the glass (7/32 inch is most common). Wrap each glass piece with the copper foil, crimp, and burnish (p29) down the edges with the lathekin or a piece of doweling.

Assembling the Panel

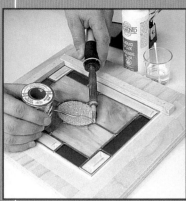

8 Arrange foiled pieces on the pattern in the jig and tack solder (p30) the pieces together.

9 Tin (p30) all exposed copper foil on the interior seams. Remember to solder no closer than 1/4 inch to the outside edge. Space must be left along the edge to allow for ease of fitting the zinc came border.

10 Bead solder (p30) the seams of the panel. Achieving a half-round raised seam will strengthen the panel and finish its appearance.

11 Turn the panel over and repeat steps 9 and 10. Since there is no right or wrong side to a stained glass panel and it is viewed from both sides, strive for even solder seams on both sides.

12 Using a pair of sidecutters or lead knippers, cut a length of zinc came for each side of the panel. Use the pattern as a guide for the length required. Cut the end of each length at a 45° angle.

13 Fit the zinc came onto the edges of the panel. If the glass is thicker than the channel in the came, use a lathekin to widen the channel. This makes it easier to fit the came around the edge of the glass. Use masking tape to hold the zinc came in place until it is soldered to the panel.

14 Solder the zinc came in place at each point it meets a solder seam on the panel and at each of the 4 corners. Repeat on opposite side of panel.

15 To make the hanging loops for the panel, wrap the tinned wire around a small cylindrical object (doweling or pencil) several times to form a coil. Slide the coil off, and using a pair of sidecutters or lead knippers, cut individual loops off the coil.

16 Place loops so that the panel hangs properly and safely. Attach the loops to a solder seam that meets with the border to prevent the border came from pulling away.

17 Clean (p33) the panel.

18 Apply finishing compound or wax (p34).

19 Use heavy monofilament line (fishing line) to hang the panel. Screw the cup hooks into the window frame and hang the panel. Suction cups are not recommended because they dry out, allowing the panel to fall and break.

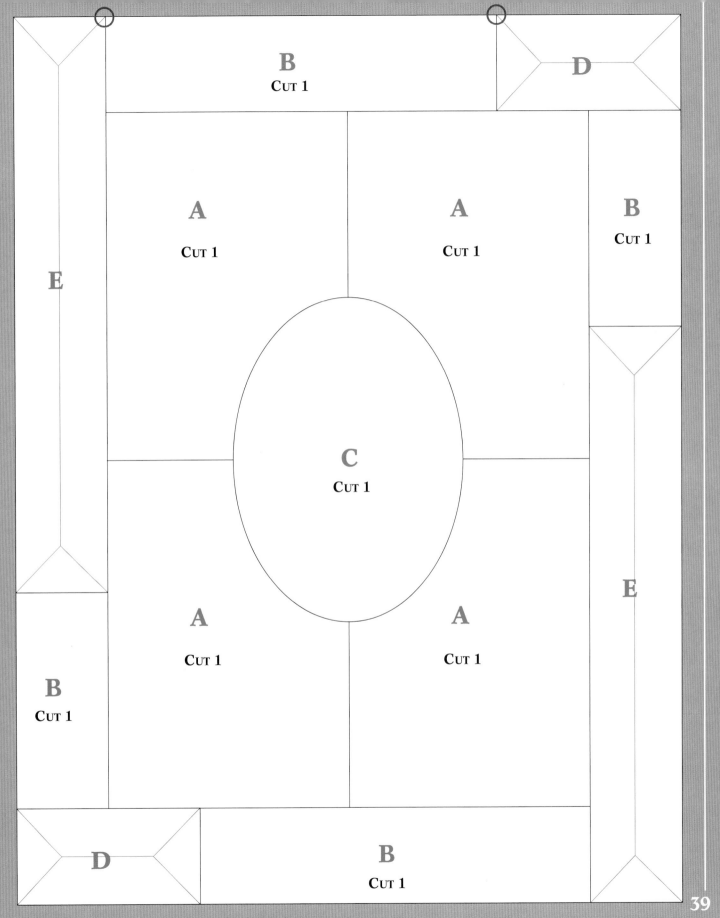

SMALL HANGING PANEL PATTERN–FULL SIZE

Peaks Hanging Panel

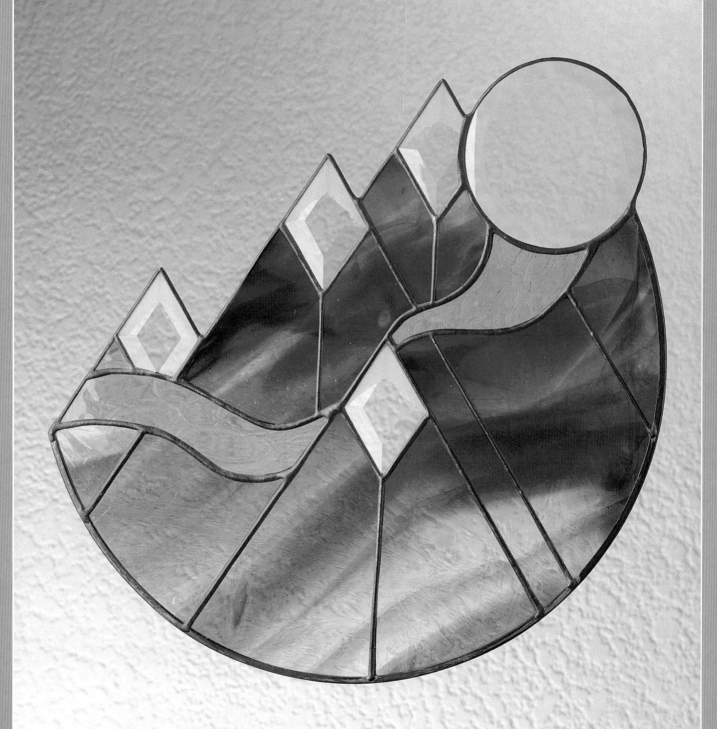

DIMENSIONS   14 in wide by 13–3/8 in high

NO. OF PIECES   19

GLASS REQUIRED

Letters refer to the type of glass used on pattern pieces (p43).

A   12 in x 14 in blue/red/amber streaky
B   5 in x 7 in amber craquel
C   4–2 in x 3 in clear diamond bevels
D   1–4 in clear circular bevel

This quantity of glass is the exact amount needed for the pattern. You may have to purchase more glass. Please allow for matching textures and grain.

MATERIALS

2 copies of pattern
Newspaper
Wood board
Masking tape
Black-backed copper foil
Safety flux
60/40 solder
1/8 in single channel U-
   shaped zinc came
18 to 20 gauge tinned
   copper wire
Neutralizing solution
Black patina
Wax or finishing compound
Heavy monofilament line
   (fishing line)

TOOLS

Apron
Safety glasses
Utility knife or scissors
Permanent waterproof fine-
   tipped marker
Cork-backed straightedge
Glass cutter
Running pliers
Breaking pliers
Glass grinder
1/4 in drilling/grinding bit
Soft cloths
Lathekin or doweling
Hammer and nails
   or push pins
Soldering iron and stand
Natural fiber sponge
Cotton swabs
Sidecutters or lead knippers
Rubber gloves
Fine steel wool (000)
Toothbrush
Cup hook screw

Preparing the Pieces

1   Follow steps 1 to 3 for Small Hanging Panel (p37).
Omit step 4.

2   Grind (p26) each piece of glass, as required, to fit the pattern.
Leave enough space between each piece so that the pattern line
(1/32 in wide) is visible between each piece. This will accommodate
the copper foil being wrapped around each piece.

3   Verify that the bevels fit the
pattern and grind to fit if they do
not (p28). As shown on the
pattern, the surface on the 2 in x
3 in diamond bevels has been
altered. With the marker, trace
(p17) the outline of the "snow
cap" onto each bevel. Grind the
pattern onto each beveled
surface by holding it at an angle
and lightly grinding, using the
1/4 in drilling/grinding bit on the
glass grinder. Practise on a piece
of scrap glass first.

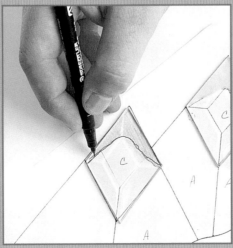

4   Follow step 7 for Small Hanging Panel (p37)
using black-backed copper foil.

Assembling the Panel

5 Tape a copy of the pattern to a wood board (slightly larger than the panel). Arrange the foiled pieces on the pattern and tack solder (p30) together. If there is concern about the pieces moving around while tacking, hold them in place with pieces of masking tape or push pins or nails around the perimeter of the panel.

6 Tin (p30) all exposed copper foil on the interior seams. Solder no closer than 1/4 in to the lower circular-shaped outside edge to allow ease of fitting the zinc came border.

7 Continue following steps 10 and 11 for Small Hanging Panel (p38).

8 Cut a 23-1/2 in length of zinc came border, to be used on the lower circular-shaped edge only. This provides support to the panel. Trim the ends at an angle to correspond with the adjoining solder seams.

9 Being careful not to kink the zinc came, slowly fit it around the lower edge of the panel. Start at the point where the circular bevel intersects with the lower outside edge. If the glass is thicker than the channel in the came, use a lathekin to widen the channel. This makes fitting easier. Use masking tape to hold the zinc came in place until it is soldered to the panel. Trim any excess zinc off the end of the lower left-hand corner.

10 Solder the zinc came in place at each point that it meets a solder seam on the panel and at the 2 ends. Repeat on the opposite side of the panel seams.

11 Tin the remaining outside edges. Bead solder (p30) each edge—make sure the solder cools before turning the project to bead the next edge.

12 Follow step 15 for Small Hanging Panel (p38).

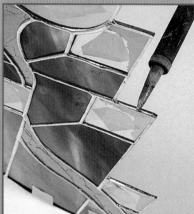

42

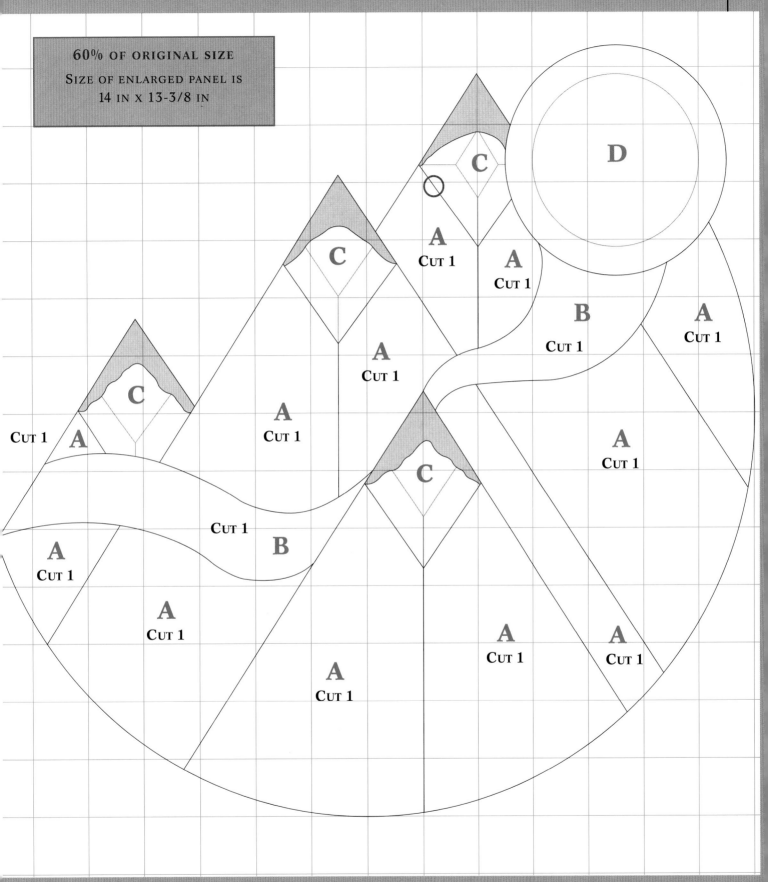

60% OF ORIGINAL SIZE
SIZE OF ENLARGED PANEL IS
14 IN X 13-3/8 IN

D

C

A
CUT 1

A
CUT 1

C

B
CUT 1

A
CUT 1

A
CUT 1

C
CUT 1

A
CUT 1

A
CUT 1

C
CUT 1

B

A
CUT 1

A
CUT 1

A
CUT 1

A
CUT 1

A
CUT 1

13 On the back of the panel, position the loop on the solder seam indicated on the pattern and solder securely in place. The loop is meant to be as inconspicuous as possible. Do not solder the loop to an outside edge.

14 Clean (p33) the panel. **15** Apply patina (p33).

16 Apply finishing compound or wax (p34).

17 Use heavy monofilament line (fishing line) to hang the panel. Screw the cup hook into the window frame and hang panel. Suction cups are not recommended because they dry out, allowing the panel to fall and break.

NOTE Because exposure to the sun's UV rays can damage the monofilament, check it occasionally and replace as needed.

GLASS REQUIRED

A 12 in x 14 in orange/brown/white/ clear streaky
B 5 in x 7 in amber craquel
C 4–2 in x 3 in diamond bevels
D 1–4 in circular bevel

Polar Bear Hanging Panel

DIMENSIONS 12-1/4 in wide by 14-1/4 in high

NO. OF PIECES 26

GLASS REQUIRED

Letters refer to the type of glass used on pattern pieces (p49).

A   3 in x 3 in orange wispy

B   6 in x 7 in white opalescent

C   4 in x 12 in white wispy

D   6 in x 12 in amber and white wispy

E   7 in x 12 in light blue cathedral

F   7 in x 10 in medium blue cathedral

G   2 in x 12 in dark blue cathedral

This quantity of glass is the exact amount needed for the pattern. You may have to purchase more glass. Please allow for matching textures and grain.

MATERIALS

2 copies of pattern
Newspaper
Wood board
Wood trim
Masking tape
Black-backed copper foil
Safety flux
60/40 solder
1/4 in single channel
   U-shaped zinc came
18 to 20 gauge tinned
   copper wire
Neutralizing solution
Black patina
Wax or finishing compound
Black sign paint
Monofilament line
   (fishing line)

TOOLS

Apron
Safety glasses
Utility knife or scissors
Permanent waterproof fine-
   tipped marker
Cork-backed straightedge
Glass cutter
Running pliers
Breaking pliers
Hammer and nails
Glass grinder
1/4 in drilling/grinding bit
Soft cloths
Lathekin or doweling
Soldering iron and stand
Natural fiber sponge
Cotton swabs
Sidecutters or lead knippers
Rubber gloves
Fine steel wool (000)
Toothbrush
Tracing brush
Cup hook screws

Preparing the Pieces

1 Follow the construction method for Small Hanging Panel (p37).

NOTE   Grind (p27) out the tight inside curve (where the ear piece fits into the front leg piece) with the 1/4 in drilling/grinding bit. Also a wider zinc came is used in this project.

The following steps are in addition to the construction method described for Small Hanging Panel.

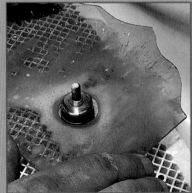

2 By making a hole in the light blue cathedral glass, the piece representing the sun can be placed in the sky without the use of unnecessary solder lines. Trace (p17) the outline of the sun onto the light blue glass piece. Wearing safety glasses and using the 1/4 in drilling/grinding bit on the grinder, drill a hole (p27) in the center of the traced sun outline on the glass. Once the initial hole is made with the drilling bit, slowly grind the opening large enough for the regular grinding bit to fit through.

3 Using the regular grinding bit, carefully grind (p26) away the glass to create a large enough opening for the sun piece.

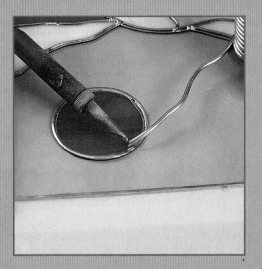

4 Copper foil the edge of the hole created in the sky piece, taking care not to tear the foil when burnishing (p29) it to the glass. Trim any excess foil where the 2 ends meet.

5 Insert the copper foiled sun piece into the opening and bead solder (p30) in place. Care must be taken not to crack the large sky piece by overheating while soldering.

Creating the detail for the Polar Bear's Ears

6 Copper foil the ear pieces. Trace the shaded portion of the pattern on the glass.

7 Apply just enough copper foil on the glass surface to cover the marked area and overlap the edge of the piece (this will help prevent the foil from lifting off the glass when the pieces are being soldered). Burnish (p29) the foil tightly to the glass. With utility knife, trim to match the pattern.

8 When the panel is being soldered, apply a bead of solder to the foil overlay, completing the detailing for the bear's ears.

Creating the Polar Bear's Claws

9 The bear's claws are pieces of tinned wire soldered to the seam of the foot. *See* pattern (p49) for placement.

Attaching the Hanging Loops

10 Because there are no solder seams intersecting with the zinc border came along the top of the panel, the loops can be soldered to the top outside corners so that the loops are attached to both the top and side pieces of the border came.

11 Clean (p33) the panel.

12 Apply patina (p33).

13 Apply finishing compound or wax (p34).

Creating the Polar Bear's Facial Features

14 Using a tracing brush and black sign paint, paint the facial detailing on the bear's glass head piece. Allow to dry.

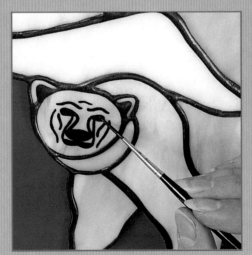

15 Screw cup hooks into the window frame. Hang the panel, using heavy monofilament line (fishing line). Suction cups are not recommended because they dry out, allowing the panel to fall and break.

NOTE
Because exposure to the sun's UV rays can damage the monofilament, check it occasionally and replace as needed.

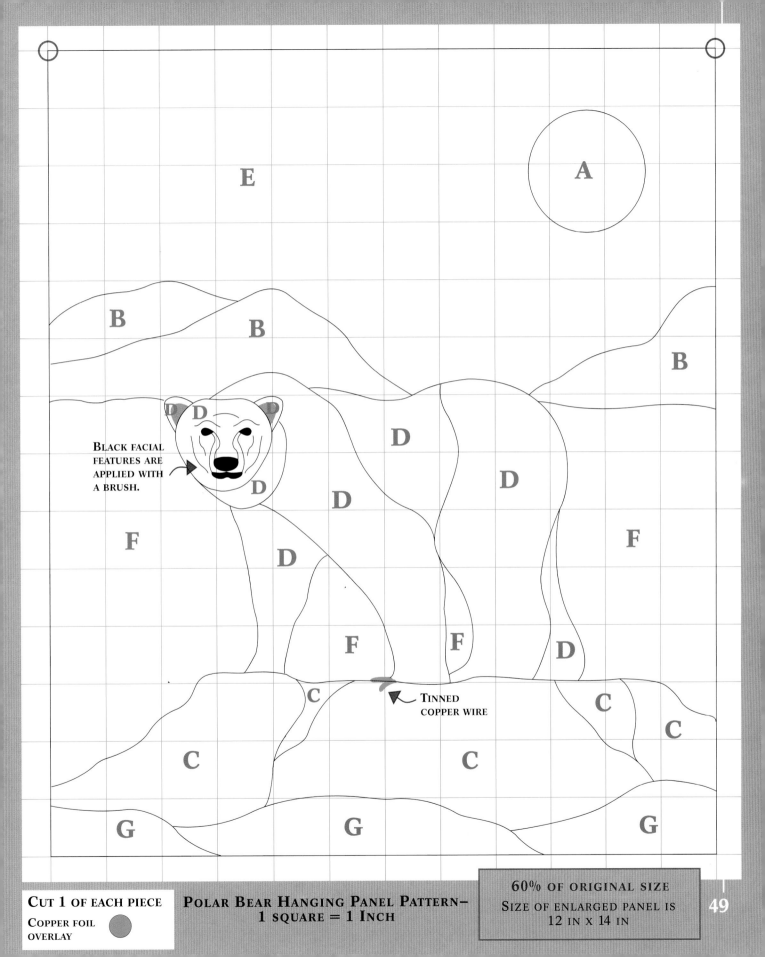

E

A

B

B

B

D D D

BLACK FACIAL
FEATURES ARE
APPLIED WITH
A BRUSH.

D

D

D

D

D

F

F

F

F

F

D

C

TINNED
COPPER WIRE

C

C

C

G

G

G

POLAR BEAR HANGING PANEL PATTERN–
1 SQUARE = 1 INCH

60% OF ORIGINAL SIZE
SIZE OF ENLARGED PANEL IS
12 IN X 14 IN

49

Thistle Hanging Panel

DIMENSIONS   9–5/8 in wide by 12–1/2 in high
NO. OF PIECES   30
GLASS REQUIRED

Letters refer to the type of glass used on pattern pieces (p53).

    A   10 in x 12 in clear textured
    B   6 in x 8 in iridescent white/clear wispy
    C   6 in x 8 in teal/white wispy
    D   2-1/2 in x 4-1/2 in violet fibroid
    E   2 in x 5 in green ripple

This quantity of glass is the exact amount needed for the pattern. You may have to purchase more glass. Please allow for matching textures and grain.

MATERIALS
2 copies of pattern
Newspaper
Wood board
Masking tape
Silver-backed copper foil
Safety flux
60/40 solder
3/16 in single channel
  U-shaped lead came
18 to 20 gauge tinned
  copper wire
Neutralizing solution
Wax or finishing compound
Monofilament line
  (fishing line)

TOOLS
Apron
Safety glasses
Utility knife or scissors
Permanent waterproof fine-
  tipped marker
Glass cutter
Running pliers
Breaking pliers
Hammer and nails or
  push pins
Glass grinder
Soft cloths
Lathekin or doweling
Soldering iron and stand
Natural fiber sponge
Cotton swabs
Lead vise
Lead knippers
Toothbrush
Cup hook screws

Preparing the Pieces

1 Follow steps 1 to 3 for Small Hanging Panel (p37).

2 Tape a copy of the pattern to a wood board (slightly larger than the hanging panel). To hold the pieces of the panel in the correct shape, use nails or push pins to form a border around the outside or tape the pieces together in strategic locations.

3 Continue following steps 5 and 7 for Small Hanging Panel (p37). Omit step 6.

Assembling the Panel

4 Making sure the pieces are properly aligned, tack solder (p30) the panel together.

5 Continue following steps 9 to 11 for Small Hanging Panel (p38).

6 Stretch lead came to eliminate any slack, making it more rigid. Place one end of came in the lead vise with the channel facing skyward. Stretch the lead came by pulling the other end of the came with a pair of pliers. The lead should stretch several inches before becoming taut. Use a smooth and even pulling motion, taking care not to pull too much and break the came.

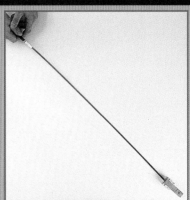

51

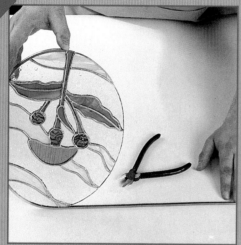

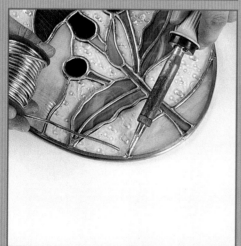

 7 Before removing the lead from the vise, verify that the panel fits into the channel. If it does not, widen the lead with a lathekin.

 8 Using the lead knippers, cut a 35-1/2 in length of lead border came.

 9 Being careful not to kink the lead came, slowly fit it around the perimeter of the panel. For a tidier edge, start one end of the lead at the bottom of the panel at a point where one of the solder seams intersects with the bottom edge. Trim excess off the end of the came so that it butts against the opposite end, achieving a nice even border.

NOTE   With the channeling facing skyward, cut the came with the flat side of the lead knippers facing away from the excess lead being cut off. Use masking tape to hold the lead came in place until it is soldered to the panel.

 10 Bead solder (p30) the lead came in place at the point where the 2 ends meet and at each location that a solder seam reaches the edge of the panel. Repeat on the opposite side of the panel.

 11 Follow steps 15 to 19 for Small Hanging Panel (p38).

NOTE   Because exposure to the sun's UV rays can damage the monofilament, check it occasionally and replace as needed.

75% OF ORIGINAL SIZE
SIZE OF ENLARGED PANEL IS
9-5/8 IN X 12-1/2 IN

THISTLE HANGING PANEL PATTERN—
1 SQUARE = 1 INCH
CUT 1 OF EACH PIECE

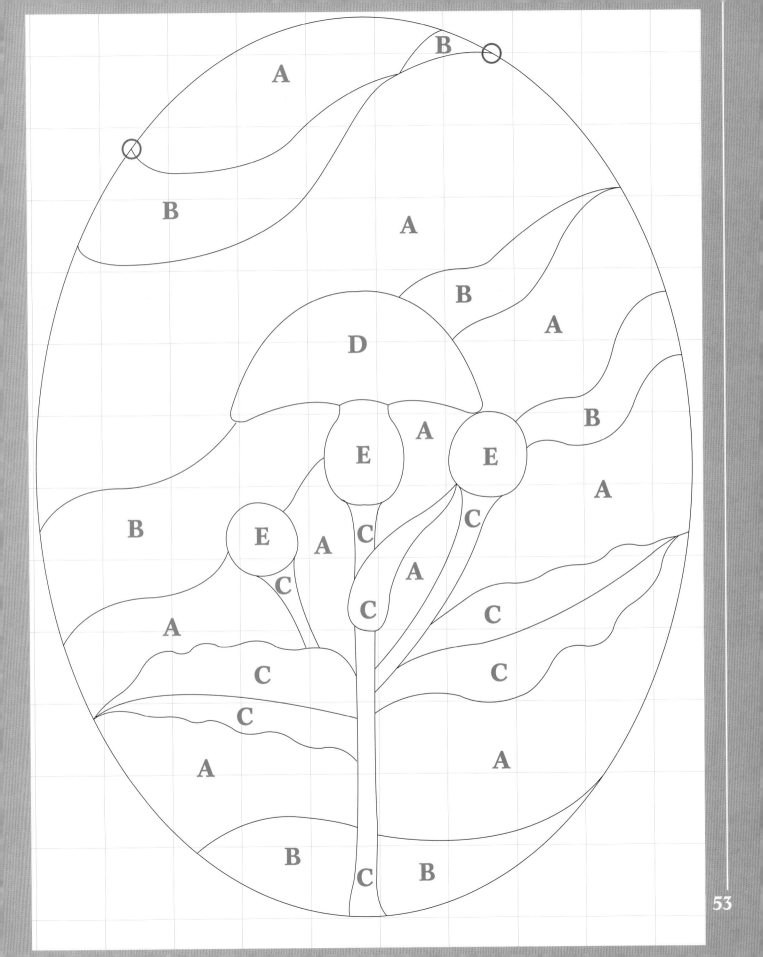

Cat Hanging Panel

DIMENSIONS   14-3/16 in diameter
No. of pieces   32
GLASS REQUIRED
Letters refer to the type of glass used on pattern pieces (p57).

A   10 in x 15 in green/yellow fractures with black streamers
B   2-1/2 in x 11 in dark green/white wispy
C   2-1/2 in x 10-1/2 in amber/white opalescent
D   10 in x 10 in dark gray/white wispy
E   8 in x 8 in pale gray/white wispy
F   2 in x 2 in dark gray cathedral
G   1 in x 1 in iridescent amber cathedral

This quantity of glass is the exact amount needed for the pattern. You may have to purchase more glass. Please allow for matching textures and grain.

MATERIALS
2 copies of pattern
Newspaper
Wood board
Masking tape
Black-backed copper foil
Safety flux
60/40 solder
1/8 in single channel
   U-shaped zinc came
18 to 20 gauge tinned
   copper wire
Neutralizing solution
Black patina
Wax or finishing compound
Monofilament line (fishing
   line)

TOOLS
Apron
Safety glasses
Utility knife or scissors
Permanent waterproof fine-
   tipped marker
Cork-backed straightedge
Glass cutter
Running pliers
Breaking pliers
Hammer and nails or
   push pins
Glass grinder
Soft cloths
Lathekin or doweling
Soldering iron and stand
Natural fiber sponge
Cotton swabs
Sidecutters or lead knippers
Rubber gloves
Fine steel wool (000)
Toothbrush
Cup hook screws

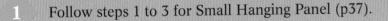

Preparing the Pieces

1   Follow steps 1 to 3 for Small Hanging Panel (p37).

2   Tape a copy of the pattern to a wood board (slightly larger than the pattern). To hold the pieces of the panel in the correct shape use nails or push pins to form a border around the outside, or tape the glass pieces together in strategic locations.

3   Continue following steps 5 and 7 for Small Hanging Panel (p37) using black-backed copper foil.

   NOTE   Foil cat's face with 3/16 in copper foil. Omit step 6.

Assembling the Panel

4   Making sure the pieces are properly aligned, tack solder (p30) the panel together.

5   Continue following steps 9 to 11 for Small Hanging Panel (p38).

6   Cut a 44-1/2 in length of zinc came with sidecutters or lead knippers.

7 Being careful not to kink the zinc came, slowly fit it around the perimeter of the panel. For a tidier edge, start one end of the zinc at the side of the panel at a point where one of the solder seams intersects with the outside edge. If the glass is thicker than the channel in the came, use a lathekin to widen the channel. This makes it easier to fit the came around the edge of the glass. Trim excess off the end of the came so that it butts against the opposite end, achieving a nice even border. Use masking tape to hold the zinc came in place until it is soldered to the panel.

8 Solder the zinc came in place at the point where the 2 ends meet and at each location that a solder seam reaches the edge of the panel. Repeat on the opposite side of the panel.

Creating the Cat's Whiskers and Eyes

9 Tinned copper wire is used for the cat's whiskers. Tack solder (p30) the wire to the panel at any point that the wire crosses a solder seam.

10 For the cat's pupils, use a longer length of wire than required and solder one end to the first seam. When the wire is securely attached at one end, cut the wire with the sidecutters at the desired length and solder the other end to the corresponding seam.

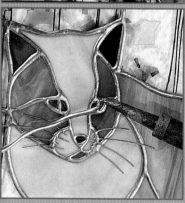

11 To add fullness to the pupils, apply flux on the middle of the wire and quickly add a drop of solder. Let it cool and repeat the process until the pupils are the desired size.

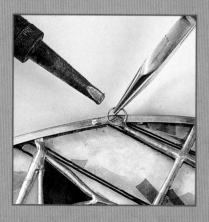

12 On the back of the panel, position the loops on the solder seams indicated on the pattern and solder securely in place.

13 Clean (p33) the panel

14 Apply patina (p33).

15 Apply finishing compound or wax (p34).

16 Screw cup hooks into the window frame. Hang the panel, using heavy monofilament line. A linked chain may be used to support the panel's weight, if desired.

NOTE   Because exposure to the sun's UV rays can damage the monofilament, check it occasionally and replace as needed.

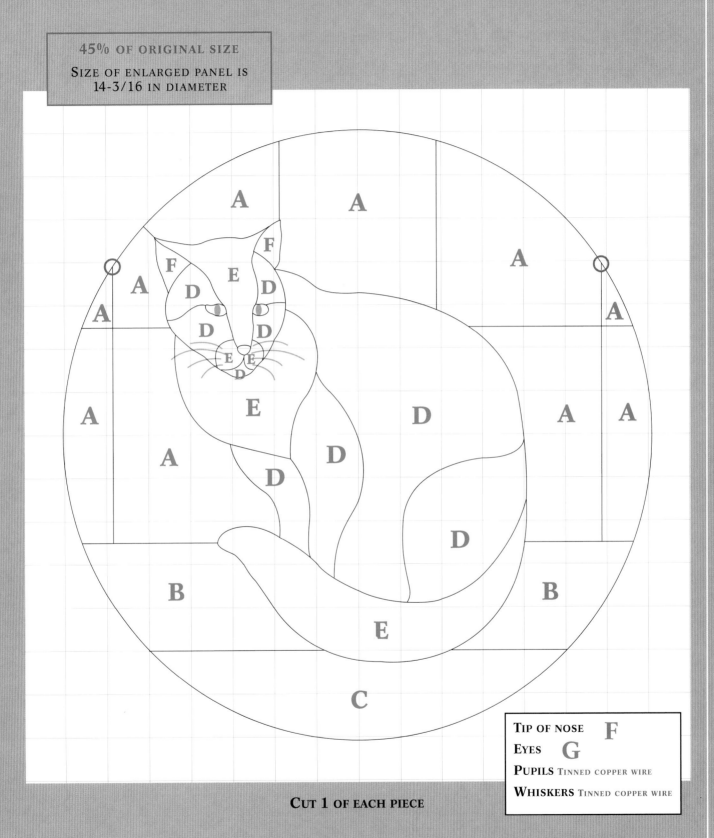

TIP OF NOSE **F**
EYES **G**
PUPILS TINNED COPPER WIRE
WHISKERS TINNED COPPER WIRE

CUT 1 OF EACH PIECE

CAT HANGING PANEL PATTERN—1 SQUARE = 1 INCH

Lamp Shade #1

DIMENSIONS Height 7-3/8 in
Bottom diameter   13-1/4 in

NO. OF PANELS 6

NO. OF PIECES 30

GLASS REQUIRED
Letters refer to the type of glass used on pattern pieces (p62).

A   6 in x 21 in ivory opalescent
B   6 in x 9 in sage green cathedral
C   3 in x 6 in brown/gold wispy
D   6 in x 7 in amber craquel
E   6–1/2 in x 1-1/2 in clear bevels

This quantity of glass is the exact amount needed for the pattern. You may have to purchase more glass. Please allow for matching textures and grain.

MATERIALS
2 copies of pattern
Wood board
Wood trim
Masking tape
Black-backed copper foil
Safety flux
60/40 solder
Electrical tape
1–3 in vase cap
Cardboard box
Newspaper
Neutralizing solution
Black patina
Wax or finishing compound
Lamp base—height 17-3/4 in

Be sure that electrical fixtures meet federal and provincial or state electrical standards and regulations.

TOOLS
Apron
Safety glasses
Utility knife or scissors
Permanent waterproof fine-tipped marker
Cork-backed straightedge
Glass cutter
Running pliers
Breaking pliers
Hammer and nails
Glass grinder
Soft cloths
Lathekin or doweling
Soldering iron and stand
Natural fiber sponge
Cotton swabs
Rubber gloves
Fine steel wool (000)
Toothbrush

Preparing the Pieces

1   Make 2 copies (p16) of each panel pattern. Use one copy as a guide for cutting and breaking the glass pieces. Use the second copy for fitting and soldering the pieces together.
NOTE   If you use opalescent glass, make a third pattern copy. Using a utility knife or scissors, cut out the necessary pieces to use as a template, remembering to cut *inside* the lines.

2   Using the marker, trace (p17) each pattern piece on the appropriate glass to be cut, paying attention to the grain of the glass.
NOTE   To avoid waste of glass used for the largest piece of the lamp shade, position the pattern pieces, as shown.

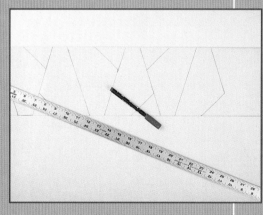

3   Cut (p18–25) each piece of glass making sure to cut *inside* the marker line.

4   Make a jig (p18) to help fit the pieces together accurately. It is important that each of the 6 panels for the lamp shade be the same size.

5   Grind (p26) each piece of glass to fit the pattern so the pattern line is visible between each piece (1/32 in wide). Rinse each piece under clean water to remove any grinding residue. Dry with a clean cloth.
NOTE   Grind and fit the pieces for one panel at a time, labeling each set with the marker. This pattern suggests the use of one bevel in each panel. Verify that the bevel fits the pattern and grind to fit if it does not (p28).

6   Choose the width of copper foil appropriate for the thickness of the glass you are using (7/32 in is most common). Wrap each glass piece with the copper foil, crimp, and burnish (p29) down the edges.

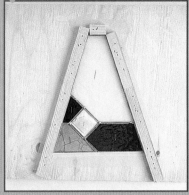

7 Arrange the foiled pieces for one panel on the pattern in the jig and tack solder (p30) the pieces together.

8 Tin (p30) all exposed copper foil on the interior seams. Remember to solder no closer than 1/4 in to the outside edge. Space must be left along the side edges to guarantee an accurate fit when the 6 panels are soldered together.

9 Bead solder (p30) the seams of the panel.

10 Turn the panel over and repeat steps 8 and 9, striving for even solder seams on both sides.

11 Tin the bottom edge of the panel and solder a finishing bead along the bottom, making sure to stay 1/4 in from the outside corners.

12 Repeat steps 7 to 11 for each of the 6 panels.

13 With a damp cloth, remove all traces of flux residue. Wipe dry with a soft cloth. Take care not to lift the exposed copper foil when cleaning.

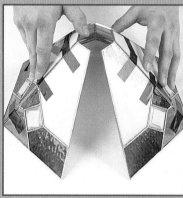

14 Lay the panels side by side on the worktable with edges touching and in proper sequence (2 mirror-image panel patterns with 3 panels each). Align the panels so that any adjoining seams as well as the bottom edges match (any small discrepancy in height can be hidden by the vase cap attached to the top of the lamp shade).

15 Cut 18 pieces of electrical tape 3 in long. Tape adjoining panels together in 3 locations.

NOTE   Use only electrical tape for this stage of construction.

16 Pull the panels up into a cone shape by slowly lifting the top edges of the panels and matching the inside edges of the 2 end panels together, top and bottom. Using the remaining 3 pieces of electrical tape, join the 2 end panels together.

17 Tack solder each adjoining edge together in several locations and where there are intersecting seams.

Adding the Vase Cap

18 With soap and water, wash off any oily residue on the vase cape. Using cotton swabs, coat the top side of cap with safety flux and apply a thin layer of solder. To get an even coating of solder, start at the top of the vase cap and slowly draw your iron tip to the bottom, repeating this process until you have gone around the entire cap. The vase cap will become very hot. Have a cloth or a pair of pliers available for safer handling. When vase cap has cooled, wash off the flux residue.

NOTE   A solid brass vase cap with several vent holes is recommended. If vented vase caps are not available, drill 6 to 8 holes in the cap.

19 Center the vase cap on the top of the lamp and solder it securely in place at each solder seam.

Finishing the Lamp Shade

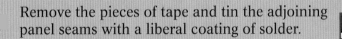

20 Remove the pieces of tape and tin the adjoining panel seams with a liberal coating of solder.

21 Fill a cardboard box, large enough to accommodate the size of the lamp shade, with crumpled newspaper. Turn the lamp shade over and prop it inside the cardboard box. Tin the 6 exposed copper foil seams.

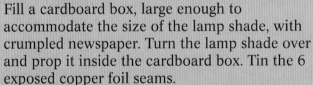

22 Bead solder (p30) the seams, making sure to join the seams to the inside of the vase cap as well. Use newspaper to prop the lamp shade at an angle that will keep the seams level while soldering. If the seam is not kept level, you will not get an even solder seam.

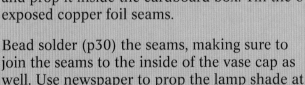

23 Turn the lamp shade over and bead solder the outside seams. Touch up any intersecting solder seams, making sure they are even and well rounded.

24 Turn the lamp shade upside down and complete the bead soldering on the adjoining bottom edges. Check the bottom edge for an even bead along the perimeter. Complete any necessary touch-ups.

25 Clean (p33) the lamp shade.

26 Apply patina (p33).

27 Apply finishing compound or wax (p34)

28 Place the finished shade on the lamp base.

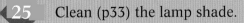

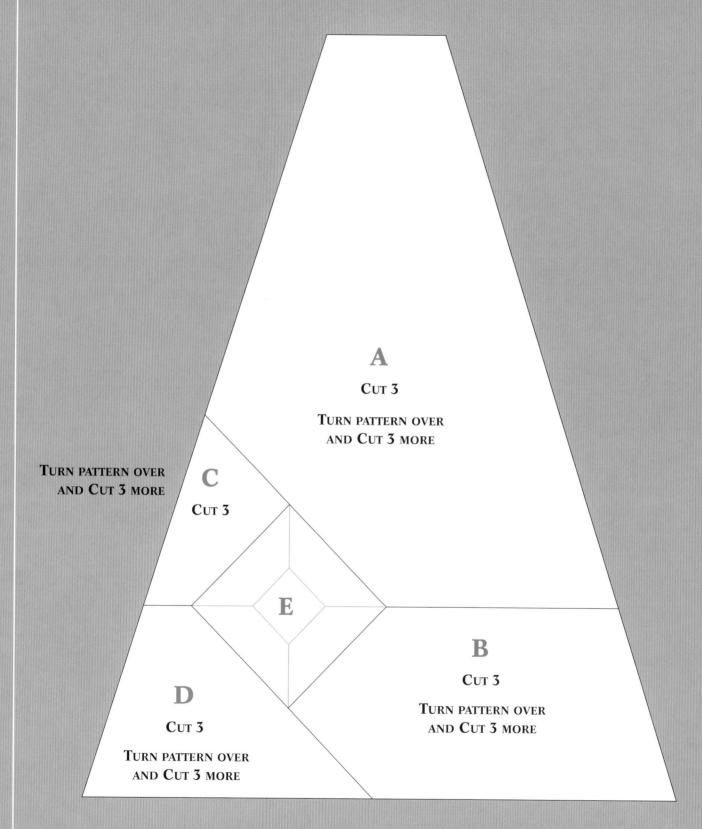

A

Cut 3

Turn pattern over
and Cut 3 more

Turn pattern over
and Cut 3 more

C

Cut 3

E

B

Cut 3

Turn pattern over
and Cut 3 more

D

Cut 3

Turn pattern over
and Cut 3 more

Lamp Shade #1 Pattern–full size

Lamp Shade #2

DIMENSIONS   Height   9-5/16 in
                 Bottom diameter   16 in
NO. OF PANELS   6
NO. OF PIECES   30
GLASS REQUIRED

Letters refer to the type of glass used on pattern pieces (p65).

A   9 in x 26-1/2 in mauve opalescent
B   10 in x 14 in blue/purple streaky
C   8 in x 12 in neo lavender cathedral
D   9 in x 13 in dark purple cathedral

This quantity of glass is the exact amount needed for the pattern. You may have to purchase more glass. Please allow for matching textures and grain.

Making the Lamp Shade

1   Assemble this lamp shade in the same way as Lamp Shade #1 (p59) but disregard the note about bevels in step 5. This pattern does not require bevels.

NOTE   Lamp shade patterns are to be reversed (turned over) to create mirror-image panels for assembly.

GLASS REQUIRED

A   9 in x 26-1/2 in green/white ring mottle
B   10 in x 14 in pink/white/clear wispy
C   8 in x 12 in clear/green translucent
D   9 in x 13 in pink/green/white fractures with black streamers

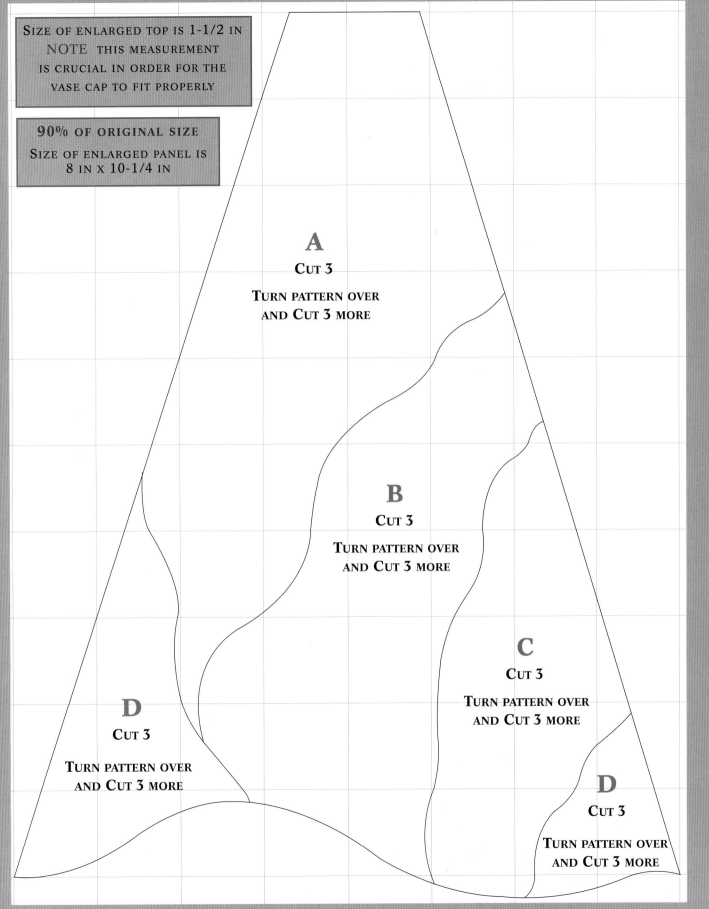

SIZE OF ENLARGED TOP IS 1-1/2 IN
NOTE THIS MEASUREMENT
IS CRUCIAL IN ORDER FOR THE
VASE CAP TO FIT PROPERLY

90% OF ORIGINAL SIZE
SIZE OF ENLARGED PANEL IS
8 IN X 10-1/4 IN

A
CUT 3
TURN PATTERN OVER
AND CUT 3 MORE

B
CUT 3
TURN PATTERN OVER
AND CUT 3 MORE

C
CUT 3
TURN PATTERN OVER
AND CUT 3 MORE

D
CUT 3
TURN PATTERN OVER
AND CUT 3 MORE

D
CUT 3
TURN PATTERN OVER
AND CUT 3 MORE

65

LAMP SHADE #2 PATTERN—1 SQUARE = 1 INCH

Lamp Shade #3

DIMENSIONS   Height   7-1/2 in
                 Bottom diameter   11-1/2 in

NO. OF PANELS   6
NO. OF PIECES   36
GLASS REQUIRED

Letters refer to the type of glass used on pattern pieces (p68).

  A   7 in x 25 in white wispy
  B   3 in x 4 in aqua wispy
  C   4 in x 14 in aqua craquel
  D   6–35mm blue smooth jewels
  E   6–20mm clear faceted jewels

This quantity of glass is the exact amount needed for the pattern. You may have to purchase more glass. Please allow for matching textures and grain.

MATERIALS
2 copies of pattern
Wood board
Wood trim
Masking tape
Black-backed copper foil
Safety flux
60/40 solder
Electrical tape
1–3 in vase cap
Cardboard box
Newspaper
Neutralizing solution
Black patina
Wax or finishing compound
Lamp base–height 15 in

Be sure that electrical fixtures meet federal and provincial or state electrical standards and regulations.

TOOLS
Apron
Safety glasses
Utility knife or scissors
Permanent waterproof fine-
    tipped marker
Cork-backed straightedge
Glass cutter
Running pliers
Breaking pliers
Hammer and nails
Glass grinder
Soft cloths
Lathekin or doweling
Soldering iron and stand
Natural fiber sponge
Cotton swabs
Rubber gloves
Fine steel wool (000)
Toothbrush

Making the Lamp Shade

1   Follow steps 1 and 2 for Lamp Shade #1 (p59).

2   Cut (pp18–25) the required glass pieces, making sure to cut inside the marked line. Some inside curves are difficult and will require several scores to break out. If you are not confident in breaking out these tight curves, cut a less severe curve and grind out the remainder (p27).

3   Follow steps 4 and 5 for Lamp Shade #1 (p59).

NOTE   Grind and fit the pieces for one panel at a time, labeling each set with the marker. This pattern uses smooth and faceted jewels in place of bevels. Cover the raised surface of the jewels with masking tape to prevent scratches (p28).

4   Continue following steps 6 to 16 for Lamp Shade #1 (p59).

5   Tack solder each adjoining edge together in several locations and where there are intersecting seams.

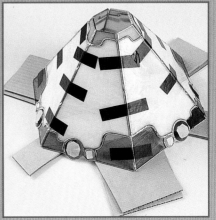

NOTE   Because the bottom edge of this lamp shade is not straight, the weight of the shade rests on the jewels. For additional support position cardboard under each adjoining panel seam, as shown.

6   Continue following steps 18 to 28 for Lamp Shade #1 (p61).

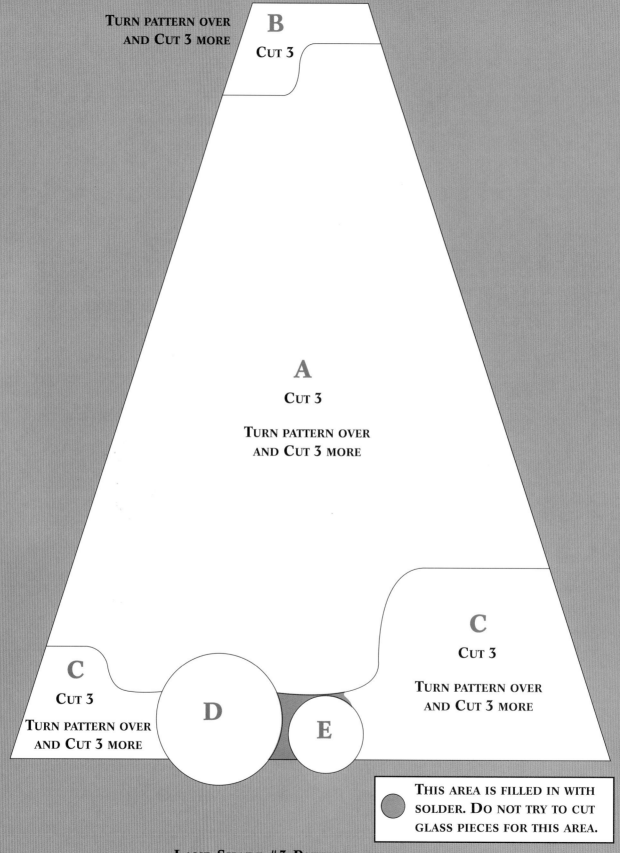

B
CUT 3

TURN PATTERN OVER
AND CUT 3 MORE

A
CUT 3

TURN PATTERN OVER
AND CUT 3 MORE

C
CUT 3

TURN PATTERN OVER
AND CUT 3 MORE

C
CUT 3

TURN PATTERN OVER
AND CUT 3 MORE

D

E

THIS AREA IS FILLED IN WITH
SOLDER. DO NOT TRY TO CUT
GLASS PIECES FOR THIS AREA.

LAMP SHADE #3 PATTERN—FULL SIZE

DIMENSIONS Height 10-3/4 in
Bottom 14-1/2 in square
NO. OF SIDES 4
NO. OF PIECES 61
GLASS REQUIRED

Letters refer to the type of glass used on pattern pieces (pp71–75).

A 15 in x 18 in orange/brown/white/clear streaky
B 14 in x 14 in clear craquel
C 12 in x 12 in rust cathedral
D 9 in x 14 in amber craquel
E 6 in x 14 in amber cathedral
F 7 in x 14 in medium brown cathedral
G 8 in x 10 in white transluscent
H 4 in x 6 in red cathedral

This quantity of glass is the exact amount needed for the pattern. You may have to purchase more glass. Please allow for matching textures and grain.

MATERIALS
2 copies of pattern
Wood board
Wood trim
Masking tape
Black-backed copper foil
Safety flux
60/40 solder
Electrical tape
18 to 20 gauge tinned copper wire
4-way spider
Cardboard box
Newspaper
Neutralizing solution
Black patina
Wax or finishing compound
"S" cluster electrical fixture

Be sure that electrical fixtures meet federal and provincial or state electrical standards and regulations.

TOOLS
Apron
Safety glasses
Utility knife or scissors
Permanent waterproof fine-tipped marker
Cork-backed straightedge
Glass cutter
Running pliers
Breaking pliers
Hammer and nails
Glass grinder
Soft cloths
Lathekin or doweling
Soldering iron and stand
Natural fiber sponge
Cotton swabs
Hacksaw or heavy gauge wire cutters
Rubber gloves
Fine steel wool (000)
Toothbrush

Preparing the Pieces

1 Follow steps 1 to 10 for Lamp Shade #1 (p59).

NOTE This pattern does not use bevels.

NOTE This lamp shade requires 2 separate jigs, one for panels 1A to 4A and one for panels 1B to 4B. Because this lamp shade is made in tiers, it is very important to make each set of panels exactly the same size.

2 Repeat steps 7 to 10 for Lamp Shade #1 for each of the 8 panels.

3 With a damp cloth, remove all traces of flux residue. Wipe dry with a soft cloth. Take care not to lift the exposed copper foil when cleaning.

Forming the Lamp Shade Body (Panels 1A to 4A)

4 Lay the panels side by side, in the correct order, on the work surface (the bottom edges should be touching). Position one of the joining pieces (piece #5 on the pattern) between each panel. Form the panels and the joining pieces into a fan shape so that there are no gaps. Align the top and bottom edges.

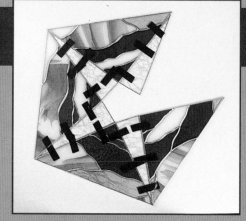

5 Cut 24–3 in pieces of electrical tape. Tape the adjoining panels and pieces together in 3 locations.

NOTE   Use only electrical tape for this stage of construction.

6 Pull up into a cone shape by slowly lifting the top edges of the panels and matching the edges of the 2 ends together, top and bottom. Using the remaining 3 pieces of electrical tape, join the 2 ends together. The bottom edges of each panel should be resting evenly on the work surface.

7 Tack solder each adjoining edge together in several locations and where there are intersecting seams.

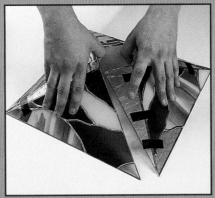 

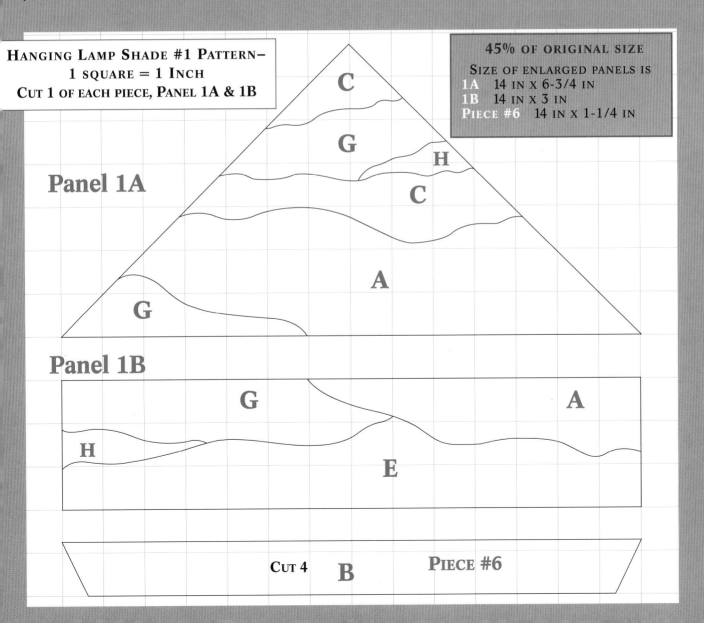

HANGING LAMP SHADE #1 PATTERN–
1 SQUARE = 1 INCH
CUT 1 OF EACH PIECE, PANEL 1A & 1B

45% OF ORIGINAL SIZE

SIZE OF ENLARGED PANELS IS
1A   14 IN X 6-3/4 IN
1B   14 IN X 3 IN
PIECE #6   14 IN X 1-1/4 IN

Panel 1A

C

G

H

C

A

G

Panel 1B

G

A

H

E

CUT 4   B   PIECE #6

8 Tin the exposed copper foil along the inside top edges of the lamp shade. Tack solder tinned copper wire around the inside of the top edge, overlapping the wire approximately 1/2 in. Place a thin layer of solder over the wire and the inside edge.

Attaching the 4-way Spider

The spider provides reinforcement and a way of hanging the lamp shade from a ceiling fixture. A solid brass spider is recommended.

9 Wash off any oily residue on the spider with soap and water.

10 Center the spider over the top opening of the lamp shade, aligning each arm of the spider with a seam. Mark the point where each arm touches the seam. Each mark should be an equal distance from the center of the spider so the lamp shade will hang properly.

11 With a hacksaw or heavy gauge wire cutter, cut each spider arm just past the mark.

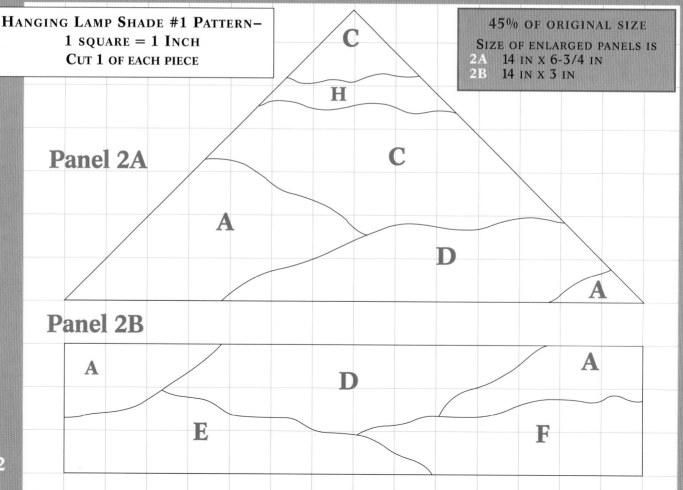

HANGING LAMP SHADE #1 PATTERN–
1 SQUARE = 1 INCH
CUT 1 OF EACH PIECE

45% OF ORIGINAL SIZE

SIZE OF ENLARGED PANELS IS
2A   14 IN X 6-3/4 IN
2B   14 IN X 3 IN

C

H

Panel 2A

C

A

D

A

Panel 2B

A

D

A

E

F

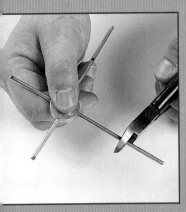

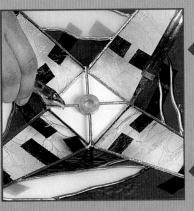

12 Carefully turn the lamp shade over. Insert the spider, making sure it is centered and that the arms are the correct length—the spider should not be able to fall through the opening. Trim the arms if required and coat the arms only with a thin layer of solder.

13 Position the spider inside the opening, making sure it is centered and the arms are aligned with a solder seam. Tack solder and then bead solder the spider arms firmly in place.

14 Tin all exposed solder seams (inside and outside) and proceed to bead solder the seams.

NOTE   Do not solder closer than 1/4 in to the top or bottom edges of the lamp shade because another tier of panels will be added to the bottom and a crown to the top.

15 To keep the seams level while soldering, fill a cardboard box (large enough to hold lamp shade) with crumpled newspaper. Prop the lamp shade with the newspaper.

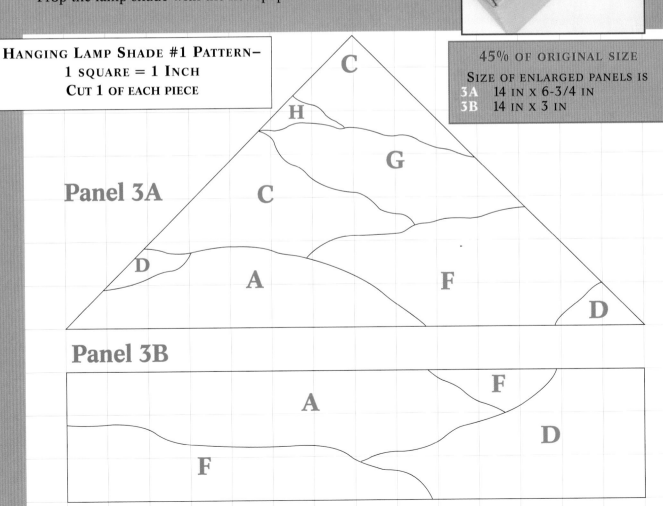

HANGING LAMP SHADE #1 PATTERN—
1 SQUARE = 1 INCH
CUT 1 OF EACH PIECE

45% OF ORIGINAL SIZE
SIZE OF ENLARGED PANELS IS
3A   14 IN X 6-3/4 IN
3B   14 IN X 3 IN

Panel 3A

Panel 3B

73

Adding the Second Tier to the Lamp Shade (Panels 1B to 4B)

For the design to flow, tack the second tier of panels to the main body of the shade in the proper sequence. Use the patterns as a guide to match the panels.

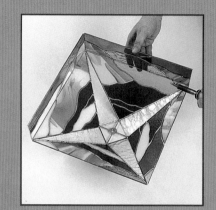

16 Position the body of the lamp shade upside down on the work surface. Starting with panel 1B, position the panel along the bottom edge of panel 1A. Make sure the panel is centered and that the inside edges and the adjoining seams of both panels are touching. The second tier of panels should be perpendicular to the work surface.

17 Tack solder into place in several locations.

18 Repeat steps 16 and 17 attaching panel 2B to 2A.

19 Align the adjoining inside edges of panels 1B and 2B and tack solder them together.

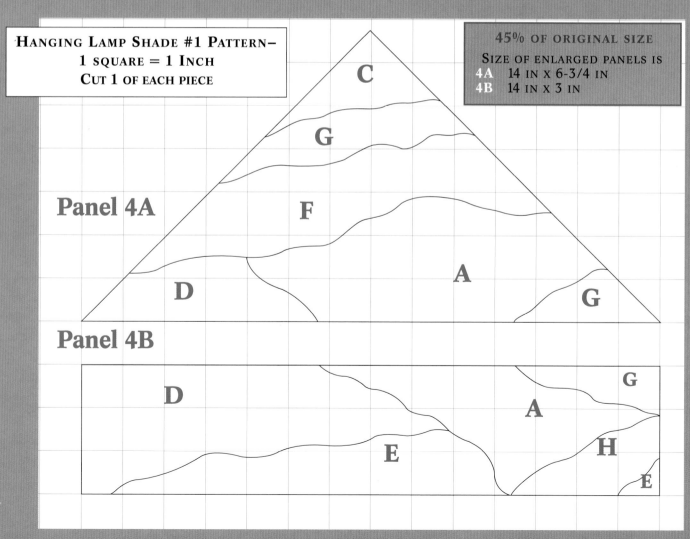

HANGING LAMP SHADE #1 PATTERN—
1 SQUARE = 1 INCH
CUT 1 OF EACH PIECE

45% OF ORIGINAL SIZE

SIZE OF ENLARGED PANELS IS
4A   14 IN X 6-3/4 IN
4B   14 IN X 3 IN

C

G

Panel 4A

F

D

A

G

Panel 4B

D

G

A

E

H

E

20 Repeat steps 16 to 19 with the remaining panels, attaching the entire second tier to the main body of the lamp shade.

21 Tin and bead solder the inside and outside seams, taking care not to solder closer than 1/4 in to the bottom edge.

Adding the Third Tier to the Second Tier

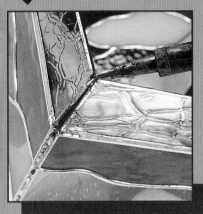

22 Use the same procedure, as described above in steps 16 to 19, to attach the third tier pieces (pattern piece 6). Angle the pieces inward instead of positioning them vertically.

23 Once the pieces are securely attached to the lamp shade, tin and bead solder all adjoining seams and the bottom edge.

Attaching the Crown

24 Use the same procedure to attach crown pieces #7 and #8 to the top opening of the lamp shade. In this case, the outside edges of the pieces should be matched up before tacking them together (the inside edges were aligned in the previous procedures).

25 Tin and bead solder all seams and the top edge of the crown.

26 Clean (p33) the lamp shade.   **27** Apply patina (p33).

28 Apply finishing compound or wax (p34).

29 Put lamp shade and "S" cluster electrical fixture together, following the manufacturer's instructions.

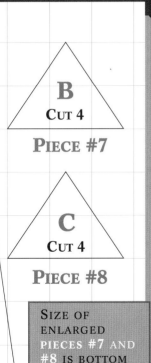

B
CUT 4
PIECE #7

C
CUT 4
PIECE #8

B
CUT 4

PIECE #5

SIZE OF ENLARGED PIECES #7 AND #8 IS BOTTOM EDGE 2-3/4 IN AND SIDES 2-3/8 IN

45% OF ORIGINAL SIZE
SIZE OF ENLARGED PIECE #5 IS BOTTOM EDGE 2-3/4 IN AND SIDES 9-5/8 IN

Hanging Lamp Shade #2

DIMENSIONS Height 10-1/4 in
                 Bottom diameter   20 in

NO. OF PANELS 6

NO. OF PIECES 36

GLASS REQUIRED
Letters refer to the type of glass used on pattern pieces (p79).

- **A** 10 in x 38 in clear texture
- **B** 11 in x 13 in blue ripple
- **C** 5 in x 6 in midnight blue cathedral
- **D** 6–2 in x 3 in clear diamond bevels

This quantity of glass is the exact amount needed for the pattern. You may have to purchase more glass. Please allow for matching textures and grain.

Be sure that electrical fixtures meet federal and provincial or state electrical standards and regulations.

MATERIALS
2 copies of pattern
Wood board
Wood trim
Masking tape
Black-backed copper foil
Safety flux
60/40 solder
Electrical tape
18 to 20 gauge tinned
   copper wire
3-way spider
1–4 in vase cap
Cardboard box
Newspaper
Neutralizing solution
Black patina
Wax or finishing compound
Swag lamp assembly

TOOLS
Apron
Safety glasses
Utility knife or scissors
Permanent waterproof fine-
   tipped marker
Cork-backed straightedge
Glass cutter
Running pliers
Breaking pliers
Hammer and nails
Glass grinder
Soft cloths
Lathekin or doweling
Soldering iron and stand
Natural fiber sponge
Cotton swabs
Sidecutters or lead knippers
Hacksaw or heavy gauge
   wire cutters
Rubber gloves
Fine steel wool (000)
Toothbrush

Making the Lamp Shade

1 Follow steps 1 to 5 for Lamp Shade #1 (p59).

2 Choose the width of copper foil appropriate for the thickness of the glass (7/32 in is most common but some ripple-textured glasses require 1/4 in copper foil). Wrap each glass piece with the copper foil, crimp, and burnish (p29) down the edges.

3 Continue following steps 7 to 10 for Lamp Shade #1 (p60). Omit step 11.

4 Continue following steps 12 to 16 for Lamp Shade #1.

5 Tack (p30) solder each adjoining edge together in several locations and where there are intersecting seams.

    NOTE Because the bottom edge of this lamp shade is not straight, the weight of the shade rests on the diamond bevels. For additional support position cardboard under each adjoining panel seam, as shown.

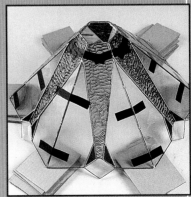

6 Because this lamp shade is larger it needs to be reinforced. Before attaching the vase cap, tin the exposed copper foil along the top edges of the lamp shade. Tack solder tinned copper wire around the inside of the top edge, overlapping the ends of the wire approximately 1/2 in. Proceed bead soldering (p30) around the entire opening.

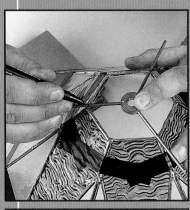

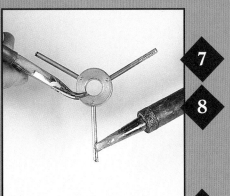

The spider provides reinforcement and a way of hanging the lamp shade from a ceiling fixture. A solid brass spider is recommended.

7 Wash off any oily residue on the spider with soap and water.

8 Center the spider over the top opening of the lamp shade, aligning each arm of the spider with a seam. Mark the point where each arm touches the seam. Each mark should be an equal distance from the center of the spider so the lamp shade will hang properly.

9 With a hacksaw or heavy gauge wire cutter, cut each spider arm just past the mark.

10 Carefully turn the lamp shade over. Insert the spider, making sure it is centered and that the arms are the correct length—the spider should not be able to fall through the opening. Trim the arms if required and coat the arms only with a thin layer of solder.

11 Position the spider inside the opening, making sure it is centered and the arms are aligned with a solder seam. Tack solder and then bead solder the spider arms firmly in place.

12 Continue following steps 18 to 23 for Lamp Shade #1 (p61).

Reinforcing the Bottom Edge

13 Reinforcement along the bottom will help support and hold this lamp shade together. Tack solder tinned copper wire along the bottom edge of the entire shade, tacking it in place at 1 in intervals. Overlap the ends of the wire approximately 1/2 in. Proceed to tin and bead solder the bottom edge. Check the bottom edge for an even bead along the perimeter and touch up as required.

14 Continue following steps 25 to 27 for Lamp Shade #1 (p61).

15 Put swag lamp assembly and lamp shade together, following the manufacturer's instructions.

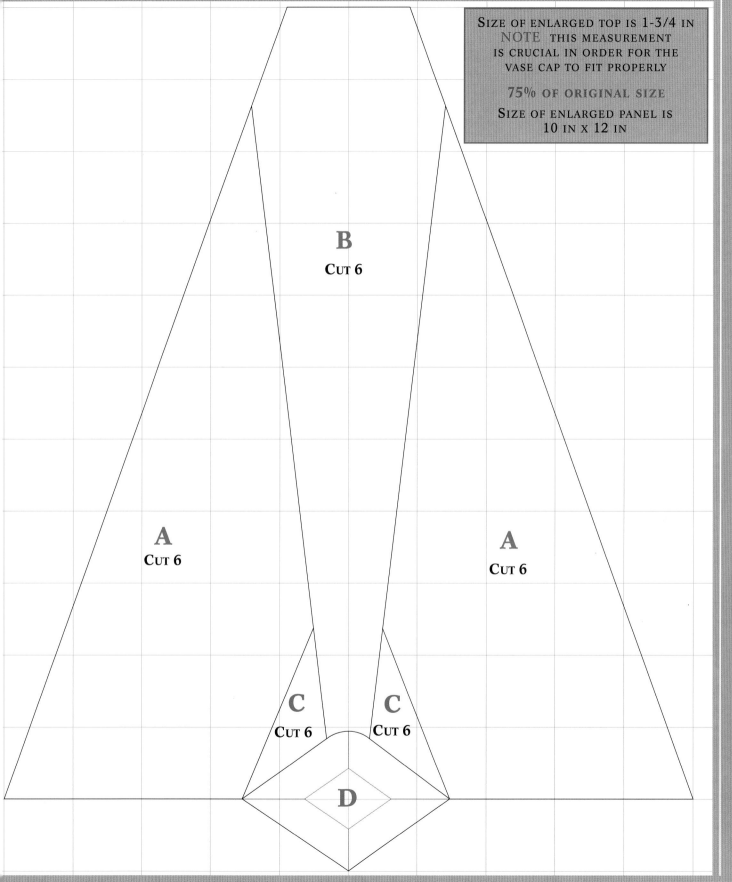

SIZE OF ENLARGED TOP IS 1-3/4 IN
NOTE THIS MEASUREMENT
IS CRUCIAL IN ORDER FOR THE
VASE CAP TO FIT PROPERLY

75% OF ORIGINAL SIZE

SIZE OF ENLARGED PANEL IS
10 IN X 12 IN

B
CUT 6

A
CUT 6

A
CUT 6

C
CUT 6

C
CUT 6

D

Decorative Dish

DIMENSIONS   diameter 13 in
NO. OF PANELS   **6**
NO. OF PIECES   31
GLASS REQUIRED
Letters refer to the type of glass used on pattern pieces (p84).

- **A**   9 in x 15-1/2 in iridescent amber cathedral
- **B**   4-1/2 in x 6 in clear textured
- **C**   3 in x 3 in violet/amber streaky cathedral
- **D**   3—iridescent lilac glass globs
- **E**   3—15mm clear faceted jewels
- **F**   3—25mm clear faceted jewels
- **G**   3—30mm purple faceted jewels

This quantity of glass is the exact amount needed for the pattern. You may have to purchase more glass. Please allow for matching textures and grain.

MATERIALS
2 copies of pattern
Wood board
Wood trim
Masking tape
Black-backed copper foil
Safety flux
60/40 solder
Electrical tape
Cardboard box
Newspaper
Neutralizing solution
Black patina
Wax or finishing compound

Because of the lead solder this project is not suitable for holding food.

TOOLS
Apron
Safety glasses
Utility knife or scissors
Permanent waterproof fine-tipped marker
Cork-backed straightedge
Glass cutter
Running pliers
Breaking pliers
Hammer and nails
Glass grinder
Soft cloths
Lathekin or doweling
Soldering iron and stand
Natural fiber sponge
Cotton swabs
Rubber gloves
Fine steel wool (000)
Toothbrush

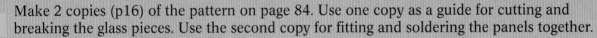

Preparing the Pieces

1 Make 2 copies (p16) of the pattern on page 84. Use one copy as a guide for cutting and breaking the glass pieces. Use the second copy for fitting and soldering the panels together.

NOTE   If you use opalescent glass make a third copy and cut out the necessary pieces (*inside* the marker lines) to use as a template.

2 Using the marker, trace (p17) each pattern piece on the glass to be cut. When placing the pattern pieces pay attention to texture or grain of the glass.

NOTE   To avoid waste, position the pattern pieces as shown.

3 Cut (pp18–25) each piece of glass inside the marker line. Use a cork-backed straightedge to assist in scoring straight lines (p22).

4 Make a jig (p18) to help fit the glass pieces together accurately. Each of the 6 panels for the dish must be the same size.

5 Grind (p26) each piece of glass as required to fit the pattern. Leave enough space between each piece (1/32 in) to accommodate the copper foil wrapped around each piece. When pieces are placed on the pattern you should be able to see the pattern line. After each piece is ground, rinse under clean water to remove any residue. Dry with a clean cloth. Grind and fit the pieces for one panel at a time, labeling each set with the marker.

NOTE   This pattern uses several different sizes of jewels and glass globs in each panel. The glass globs are irregular in shape. Select 3 that fit closest to the pattern. Grind jewels to fit. (*See* How to Prepare Beveled Glass, p28.)

6 Choose the width of copper foil appropriate for the thickness of the glass you are using (7/32 in copper foil is the most common but the jewels may require 3/16 in). Wrap each glass piece with the copper foil, crimp, and burnish (p29) down the edges.

Assembling the Panel

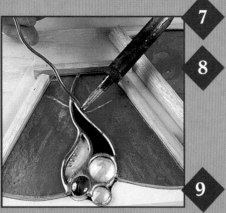

7 Arrange the foiled pieces (for one panel) on the pattern in the jig and tack solder (p30) the pieces together.

8 Tin (p30) all exposed copper foil on the interior seams. Remember to solder no closer than 1/4 in to the bottom edge of the panel. A flat seam must be left along the bottom edge to guarantee an accurate fit when the 6 panels are soldered together and the base is attached to form the dish.

9 Bead solder (p30) the seams of the panel.

10 Turn the panel over and repeat steps 8 and 9, striving for even solder seams on both sides.

11 Tin the top edge of the panel on both sides and apply decorative "splatter" soldering.

Applying Decorative Solder

Be sure to wear safety glasses for this procedure.

12 Apply a generous amount of solder to the edge. While the solder is still molten use a cotton swab soaked with safety flux to "push" the solder into a design. Keep adding and reheating the solder and applying the flux-soaked cotton swab until the desired effect is accomplished. Practise on a piece of foiled scrap glass before attempting the panels for the dish. Leave 1/4 in from the outside edges free of solder until the 6 panels are assembled. Place decorative solder around the jewels and glass globs, allowing glass to cool occasionally to prevent heat cracks.

13 Repeat steps 7 to 12 for each of the 6 panels.

14 With a damp cloth, remove all traces of flux residue. Wipe dry with a soft cloth. Take care not to lift the exposed copper foil when cleaning.

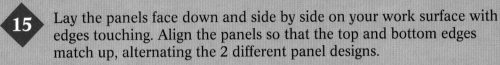

Forming Panels into a Dish

15 Lay the panels face down and side by side on your work surface with edges touching. Align the panels so that the top and bottom edges match up, alternating the 2 different panel designs.

NOTE If there is any discrepancy in the height of the panels, make sure it is the bottom edges that are lined up evenly.

16 Cut 18 pieces of electrical tape, approximately 3 in long. Tape the adjoining panels together in 3 locations.

NOTE Use only electrical tape for this stage of construction.

17 Pull up into a cone shape by slowly lifting the bottom edges of the panels and matching the edges of the 2 ends together, top and bottom. Using the remaining 3 pieces of electrical tape, join the 2 ends together. The top edges of each panel should be resting evenly on the work surface.

18 Tack solder each adjoining edge together in several locations.

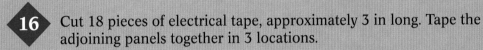

Attaching the Base

19 Tin the top and bottom sides of the base piece, making sure there are no bumps in the solder that will interfere with a proper fit.

20 Place the base onto the dish, aligning the corners with the adjoining seams of the panels and tack solder into place. Tack at corners as well as at several places along the seams.

21 Remove the pieces of tape and tin the adjoining panel and base seams with a liberal coating of solder.

22 Fill a cardboard box, large enough to accommodate the size of the dish, with crumpled newspaper. Turn the dish over and prop it inside the cardboard box. Tin all exposed copper foil seams.

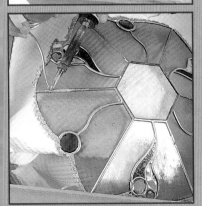

23 Bead solder the seams, making sure to join the seams to the inside of the base as well. Use newspaper to prop the dish at an angle that will keep the seams level while soldering. If the seam is not kept level, it will be difficult to achieve an even solder seam.

24 Turn the dish over and bead solder the outside seams.

25 Turn the dish right side up and complete the decorative soldering on the adjoining top edges. Check the top edge and make any touch-ups required along the perimeter.

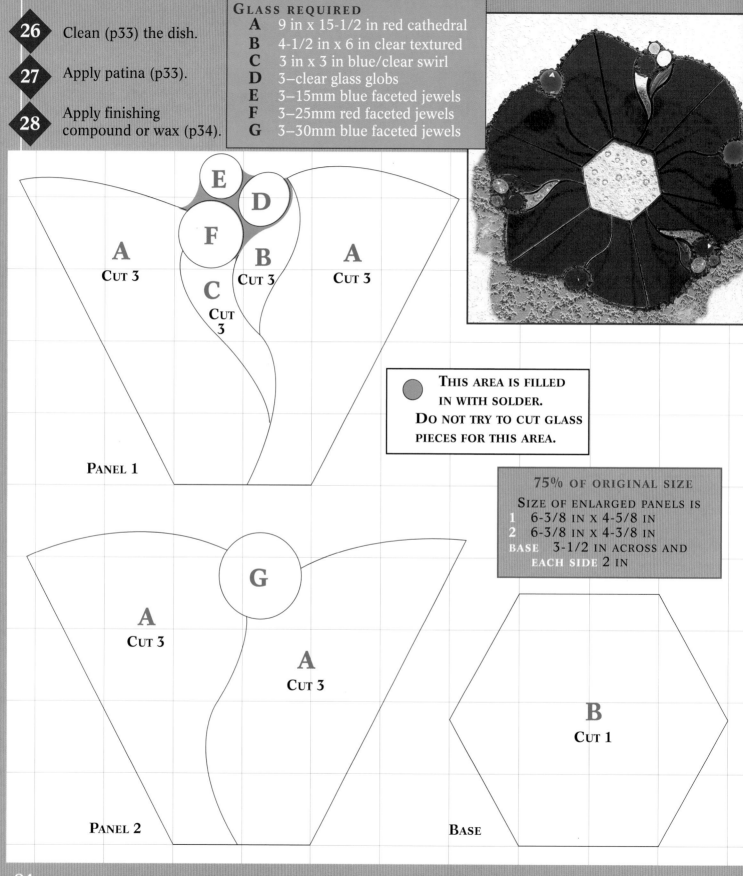

26 Clean (p33) the dish.

27 Apply patina (p33).

28 Apply finishing compound or wax (p34).

GLASS REQUIRED
A	9 in x 15-1/2 in	red cathedral
B	4-1/2 in x 6 in	clear textured
C	3 in x 3 in	blue/clear swirl
D	3—clear glass globs	
E	3—15mm	blue faceted jewels
F	3—25mm	red faceted jewels
G	3—30mm	blue faceted jewels

E

D

F

B

A
CUT 3

C
CUT 3

A
CUT 3

PANEL 1

THIS AREA IS FILLED
IN WITH SOLDER.
DO NOT TRY TO CUT GLASS
PIECES FOR THIS AREA.

75% OF ORIGINAL SIZE
SIZE OF ENLARGED PANELS IS
1 6-3/8 IN X 4-5/8 IN
2 6-3/8 IN X 4-3/8 IN
BASE 3-1/2 IN ACROSS AND
EACH SIDE 2 IN

G

A
CUT 3

A
CUT 3

PANEL 2

B
CUT 1

BASE

DECORATIVE DISH PATTERN—1 SQUARE = 1 INCH

Hinged Box #1

DIMENSIONS   6-1/4 in wide by 2-3/8 in high
by 4-1/2 in deep

NO. OF PIECES   14

GLASS REQUIRED
Letters refer to the type of glass used on pattern pieces (p89).

A   3-1/4 in x 6-1/2 in teal/white wispy
B   4 in x 4 in rose ripple
C   1–1 in x 1 in teal faceted jewel
D   3–1 in x 1 in clear bevels
E   2–2 in x 4 in clear bevels
F   2–2 in x 6 in clear bevels
G   1–4-1/16 in x 6-1/16 in 3mm mirror

This quantity of glass is the exact amount needed for the pattern. You may have to purchase more glass. Please allow for matching textures and grain.

MATERIALS
2 copies of pattern
Wood board
Wood trim
Masking tape
Black-backed copper foil
Safety flux
60/40 solder
Clear nail polish
Cardboard box
Newspaper
Rod and tube hinge assembly
Wooden toothpicks
7 in fine-linked chain
Neutralizing solution
Black patina
Wax or finishing compound

TOOLS
Apron
Safety glasses
Utility knife or scissors
Permanent waterproof fine-tipped marker
Cork-backed straightedge
Glass cutter
Running pliers
Breaking pliers
Hammer and nails
Glass grinder
Soft cloths
Lathekin or doweling
Soldering iron and stand
Natural fiber sponge
Cotton swabs
Small file
Sidecutters or lead knippers
Needle-nose pliers
Rubber gloves
Fine steel wool (000)
Toothbrush

Preparing the Pieces

1   Make 2 copies (p16) of the pattern (p89). Use one copy as a guide for cutting and breaking the glass pieces. Use the second copy for fitting and soldering the lid together.

NOTE   If you are using opalescent glass, make a third copy and cut out the necessary pieces to use as a template.

2   Using the marker, trace (p17) each pattern piece on the glass to be cut. Place the pattern pieces so that the texture and grain of the glass are taken into account.

3   Cut (pp18–25) each piece of glass inside the marker line. Use the cork-backed straightedge to assist in scoring straight lines (p22). Cut the mirror (p28).

Making the Lid

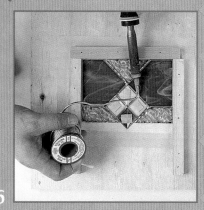

4   Make a jig (p18) to help fit the glass pieces together accurately.

5   Grind (p26) each piece of glass to fit the pattern, leaving 1/32 in width between each piece so that the pattern line is clearly visible. Rinse each piece under clean water to remove any grinding residue and dry with a clean cloth.

NOTE   Verify that the bevels fit the pattern and grind to fit if they do not (p28).

6   Choose the width of copper foil (7/32 in is most common) appropriate for the thickness of the glass you are using. Wrap each glass piece with the copper foil, crimp, and burnish (p29) down the edges.

7   Arrange foiled pieces on the pattern in the jig and tack solder (p30) the pieces together.

8	Tin (p30) all exposed copper foil.
9	Bead solder (p30) all the seams on the lid. Turn the lid over and repeat the soldering procedure.
10	Prop lid on edge and tin and bead solder the front and 2 side edges. The back edge of the lid where the hinge will go should be tinned only, do not bead.

Making the Box

	Pre-cut bevels are used for the sides of the box in this pattern.
11	Verify that the bevels fit the pattern and grind to fit if they do not (p28).
12	Prepare the mirror for the bottom of the box (p28).
13	To assemble the box, bring together 2 side pieces (one 2 in x 4 in bevel and one 2 in x 6 in bevel), as shown, so inside edges are touching and are at a right angle to each other and the mirrored bottom. Tack solder (p30) together.
14	Bring together and tack the remaining 2 side pieces, as above.
15	Bring the 2 halves together and tack at the top and bottom edges.
16	Tin the inside seams of the box.
17	Tin the copper foil on the mirrored bottom piece.
18	Position the mirrored bottom onto the tacked side pieces and tack solder in place.
19	Tin all exposed copper foil.
20	Fill a cardboard box with crumpled newspaper to hold the glass box at an appropriate angle for soldering.
21	Bead solder all seams except the 2 rear corner seams where the hinge will be placed. Keep the seams level as they are being soldered.
22	Bead solder the top edges of the box, taking care not to solder in the 2 rear corner edges where the hinge will be placed.

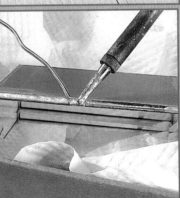
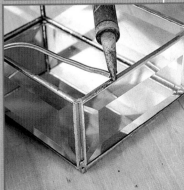

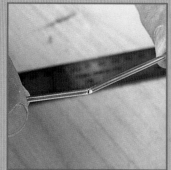

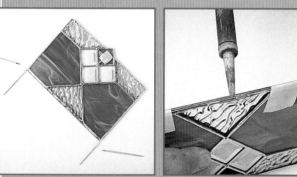

23 Remove the rod from the tube. Using the edge of a small file, score a notch in the tube to make the length of the tube 5-15/16 in.

24 Hold the tube in both hands with the score facing away from the body. Snap the tube. Remove any burrs with the file. Place wooden toothpicks in each end.

25 Tin the tube, but do not solder over the ends of the tube.

26 Using the sidecutters or lead knippers, cut 2–3-3/4 in lengths of rod.

27 Bend each rod piece in half to form right angles.

28 Center and tack tinned tube to the back edge of the lid. Bead solder tube in place, but do not solder ends of the tube. Keep toothpicks in place while soldering.

29 Remove the toothpicks and set the 2 rod pieces into the ends of the tube on the lid.

30 Place pieces of scrap paper between the lid and the top edge of the box. Tack the 2 rod pieces into the 2 unsoldered rear corners. Remove scrap paper and operate lid to ensure freedom of movement.

31 Bead solder the corners. Slightly angle the box, as shown, to prevent solder from running toward hinge assembly.

32 Lay box on its side and solder one end of the chain to the bottom front corner. Use a pair of needle-nose pliers to hold the chain in place. Bend lid to the maximum openness desired. Place other end of chain 1/2 in from outside edge on a solder seam. Mark and cut chain with sidecutters or lead knippers.

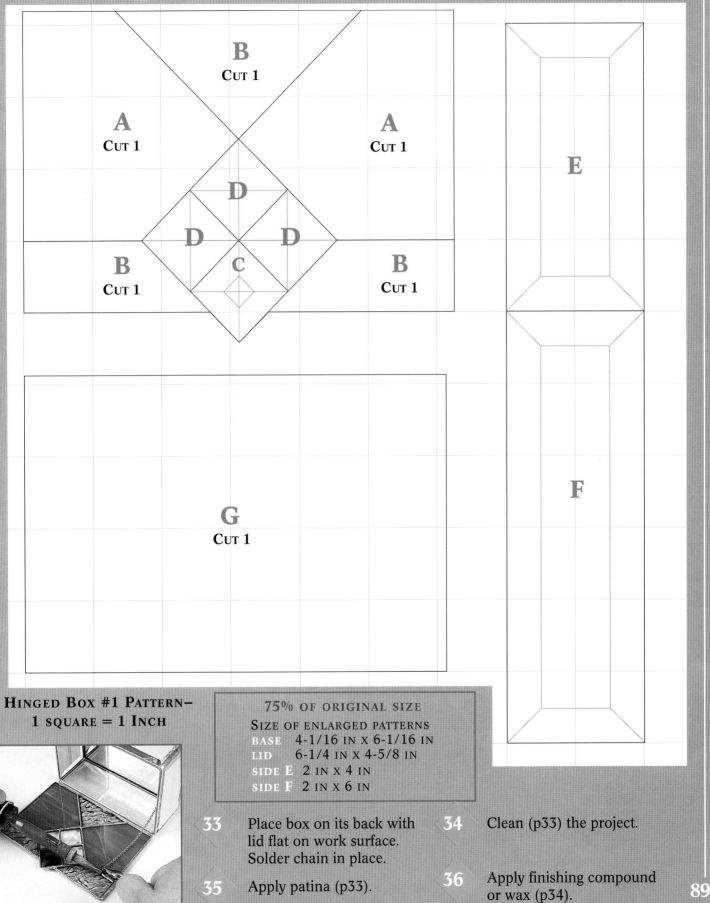

B
CUT 1

A
CUT 1

A
CUT 1

D

D   D

B
CUT 1

C

B
CUT 1

E

F

G
CUT 1

**HINGED BOX #1 PATTERN–
1 SQUARE = 1 INCH**

33   Place box on its back with lid flat on work surface. Solder chain in place.

34   Clean (p33) the project.

35   Apply patina (p33).

36   Apply finishing compound or wax (p34).

Hinged Box #2

DIMENSIONS 6-1/4 in wide by 2-3/8 in high
by 4-1/2 in deep

NO. OF PIECES 12

GLASS REQUIRED

Letters refer to the type of glass used on pattern pieces (p91).

- **A** 6-1/4 in x 11-1/2 in white wispy
- **B** 3 in x 3-1/4 in aqua craquel
- **C** 2 in x 3 in aqua wispy
- **D** 1–20mm clear faceted jewel
- **E** 1–35mm blue smooth jewel
- **F** 1–4-1/16 in x 6-1/16 in 3mm mirror

This quantity of glass is the exact amount needed for the pattern. You may have to purchase more glass. Please allow for matching textures and grain.

MATERIALS
2 copies of pattern
Wood board
Wood trim
Masking tape
Black-backed copper foil
Safety flux
60/40 solder
Clear nail polish
Cardboard box
Newspaper
Rod and tube hinge assembly
Wooden toothpicks
7 in fine-linked chain
Neutralizing solution
Black patina
Wax or finishing compound

TOOLS
Apron
Safety glasses
Utility knife or scissors
Permanent waterproof fine-tipped marker
Cork-backed straightedge
Glass cutter
Running pliers
Breaking pliers
Hammer and nails
Glass grinder
Soft cloths
Lathekin or doweling
Soldering iron and stand
Natural fiber sponge
Cotton swabs
Small file
Sidecutters or lead knippers
Needle-nose pliers
Rubber gloves
Fine steel wool (000)
Toothbrush

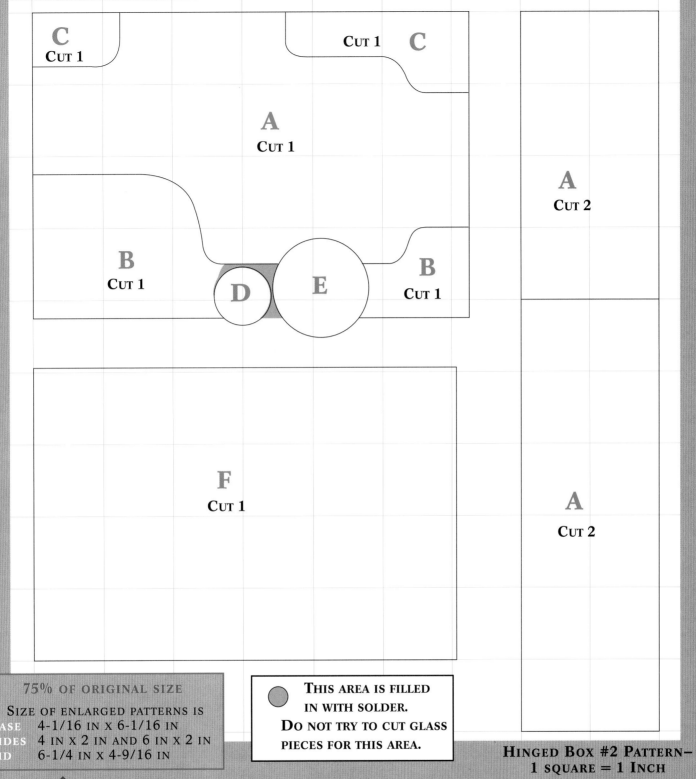

C
CUT 1

CUT 1   C

A
CUT 1

A
CUT 2

B
CUT 1

D   E

B
CUT 1

F
CUT 1

A
CUT 2

THIS AREA IS FILLED
IN WITH SOLDER.
DO NOT TRY TO CUT GLASS
PIECES FOR THIS AREA.

HINGED BOX #2 PATTERN–
1 SQUARE = 1 INCH

1 Follow the same construction and assembly instructions as used for Hinged Box #1 (p86).

NOTE   White glass is used for the sides of the box in place of bevels. There are several tight inside curves in this pattern. It may be easier to grind with a 1/4 in drilling/grinding bit (p27) instead of trying to break them out with the breaking pliers.

Triangular Hinged Box with Ring Holder

DIMENSIONS   4-3/8 in wide by 4-3/16 in high by 3-3/4 in deep

NO. OF PIECES   10

GLASS REQUIRED

Letters refer to the type of glass used on pattern pieces (p95).

   A   3–3 in x 3 in x 4-1/4 in clear triangular bevels
   B   3–2 in x 4 in clear rectangular bevels
   C   1–4 in x 4-1/2 in 3mm mirror
   D   1–3-1/2 in x 7-1/2 in rose craquel

This quantity of glass is the exact amount needed for the pattern. You may have to purchase more glass. Please allow for matching textures and grain.

MATERIALS

1 copy of pattern
Clear nail polish
Silver-backed copper foil
Masking tape
Safety flux
60/40 solder
Cardboard box
Newspaper
Rod and tube hinge assembly
Wooden toothpicks ·
14 gauge tinned copper wire
Neutralizing solution
Wax or finishing compound

TOOLS

Apron
Safety glasses
Utility knife or scissors
Permanent waterproof fine-tipped marker
Cork-backed straightedge
Glass cutter
Running pliers
Breaking pliers
Glass grinder
Soft cloths
Lathekin or doweling
Soldering iron and stand
Natural fiber sponge
Cotton swabs
Small file
Sidecutters or lead knippers
Small square
Needle-nose pliers
Rubber gloves
Fine steel wool (000)
Toothbrush

Preparing the Pieces

1 Follow steps 1 to 3 of Hinged Box #1 (p86). Make only one copy (p16) of the pattern (p95).

2 Grind (p26) each piece of glass, as required, to fit the pattern. After each piece is ground, rinse under clean water to remove any grinding residue and dry with a clean cloth.

3 This pattern uses clear bevels. Verify that the bevels fit the pattern and grind to fit if they do not (p28).

4 Prepare the mirror for the bottom of the box (p28).

5 Choose the width of copper foil (7/32 in is most common) appropriate for the thickness of glass you are using. Wrap each glass piece with the copper foil, crimp and burnish (p29) down the edges.

Making the Lid

6 Tin (p30) all exposed copper foil on the back side of the 3 triangular bevels. Wipe off excess flux with a damp cloth and dry.

7 Placing the bevels face down on the work surface, align the side edges of the bevels so they touch, as shown. Use masking tape to hold them in position.

8 Turn the bevels over and form into a pyramid. Make sure the sides of each bevel touch along their inside edges. Tape the remaining seam together.

9 Tack (p30) solder the adjoining seams together.

10 Tin and bead (p30) solder all the seams on the outside of the lid. Turn the lid over and repeat the soldering procedures on the inside seams. Prop lid on crumpled newspaper inside a small cardboard box to keep seams level while bead soldering.

11 Tin all 3 bottom edges.

12 Bead solder 2 of the bottom edges. Do not bead solder the back edge of the lid where the hinge will go.

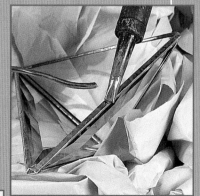

Making the Box

13 To assemble box, bring together the 3 rectangular side pieces, as shown, so the inside edges are touching. Tape together. The inside edges of the bevels should be aligned.

14 Tack solder at the top and bottom edges.

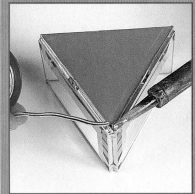

15 Tin the inside seams of the box.

16 Tin the copper foil on the mirrored bottom piece.

17 Position the mirrored bottom piece on the tacked side pieces and tack solder in place.

18 Tin all exposed copper foil.

19 Bead solder all seams with the exception of the 2 rear corner seams where the hinge will be placed. Use the cardboard box filled with newspaper to keep the seams level as they are being soldered.

20 Bead solder the top edges of the sides of the box, taking care not to get solder in the 2 rear corner edges where the hinge will be placed.

NOTE   Do not bead solder the top edge of the back of the box.

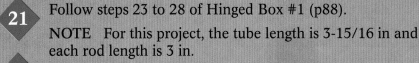

Attaching the Hinge

21 Follow steps 23 to 28 of Hinged Box #1 (p88).

NOTE   For this project, the tube length is 3-15/16 in and each rod length is 3 in.

22 Place the bend and one end of the rod into the jaws of the pliers. Grasping the pliers firmly, bend the other end of the rod downward at a 23° angle (approximate). Repeat the procedure with the other piece of bent rod.

23 Follow steps 29 to 31 of Hinged Box #1.

Making the Ring Holder

24 Follow steps 5 to 10 to make and assemble the ring holder for the inside of the box.

25 Bead solder all 3 bottom edges.

26 With a pair of sidecutters or lead knippers, cut 3–1-1/4 in lengths of tinned copper wire.

27 Using the needle-nose pliers, form a hook at each end of the wires.

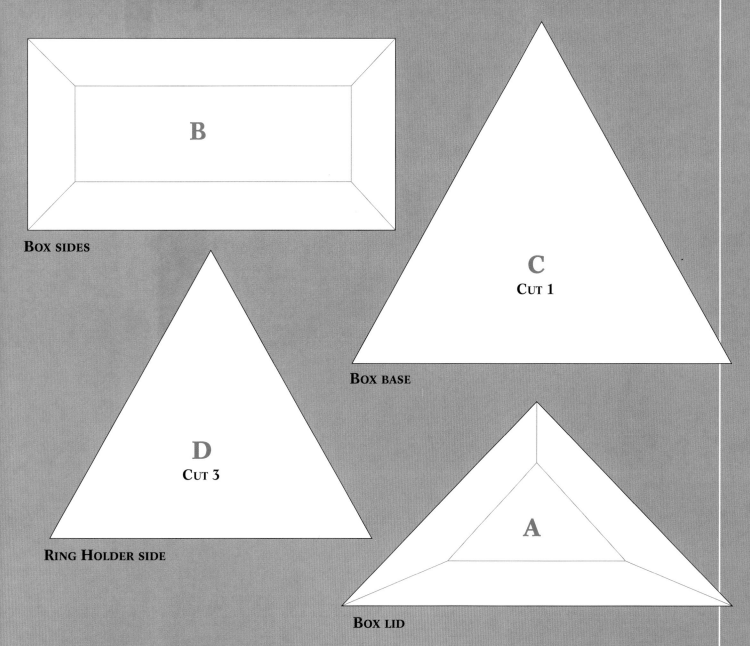

B

BOX SIDES

C
CUT 1

BOX BASE

D
CUT 3

RING HOLDER SIDE

A

BOX LID

TRIANGULAR HINGED BOX WITH RING HOLDER PATTERN–FULL SIZE

28 Tack solder one end of each wire to the peak of the ring holder.

29 Tape the lower portion of the wires to the glass so that the wires will not detach when bead soldering.

30 Bead solder the point where the wires meet. Remove masking tape.

31 Clean (p33) the project.

32 Apply finishing compound or wax (p34).

33 Place ring holder inside box.

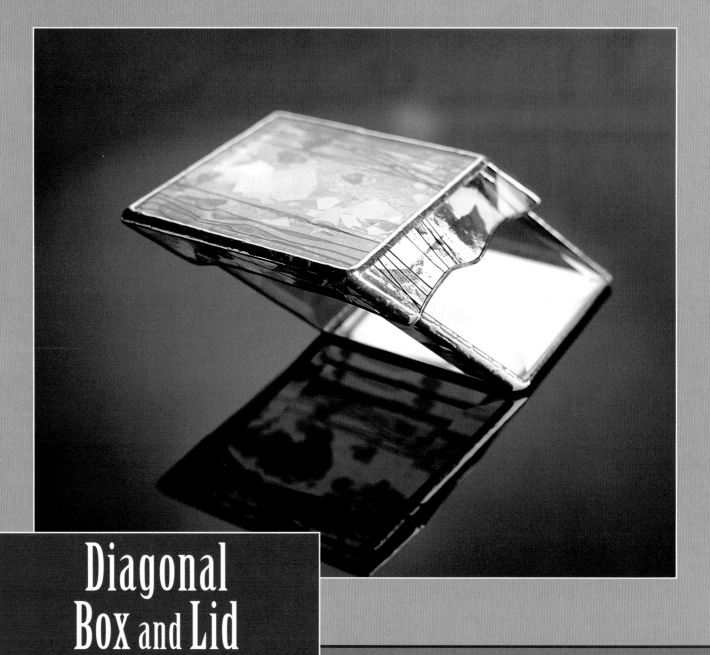

Diagonal Box and Lid

DIMENSIONS 6-3/4 in wide by 3-1/16 in high by 9-1/4 in deep

NO. OF PIECES 10

GLASS REQUIRED

Letters refer to the type of glass used on pattern pieces (p98).

A 5-1/2 in x 11 in pink/plum/white fractures with black streamers

B 4–4 in x 7 in clear diamond bevels

C 1–4 in x 4 in 3mm mirror

This quantity of glass is the exact amount needed for the pattern. You may have to purchase more glass. Please allow for matching textures and grain.

MATERIALS
1 copy of pattern
Masking tape
Clear nail polish
Silver-backed copper foil
Safety flux
60/40 solder
Cardboard box
Newspaper
Neutralizing solution
Wax or finishing compound

TOOLS
Apron
Safety glasses
Utility knife or scissors
Permanent waterproof fine-tipped marker
Cork-backed straightedge
Glass cutter
Running pliers
Breaking pliers
Glass grinder
Soft cloths
Lathekin or doweling
Soldering iron and stand
Natural fiber sponge
Cotton swabs
Toothbrush

Preparing the Pieces

1 Make one copy(p16) of the pattern (p98).

NOTE If you are using opalescent glass, make a second pattern copy. Cut out the necessary pieces to use as a template, remembering to cut inside the pattern lines.

2 Using the marker, trace (p17) each pattern piece that needs to be cut, onto the glass. Place the pattern pieces so that any texture or grain of the glass is taken into account.

3 Cut (pp18–25) each piece of glass, as required, making sure to cut inside the line. Use the cork-backed straightedge to assist in scoring straight lines (p22).

NOTE Cut the mirror (p28).

4 Grind (p26) each piece of glass, as required, to fit the pattern. After each piece is ground, rinse under clean water to remove any grinding residue. Dry with a clean cloth.

5 This pattern uses clear bevels. Verify that the bevels fit the pattern and grind to fit if they do not (p28).

6 Prepare the mirror for the bottom of the box (p28).

7 Choose the width of copper foil (7/32 in is most common) appropriate for the thickness of glass you are using. Wrap each glass piece with copper foil, crimp, and burnish (p29) down the edges.

Making the Box

8 Tin (p30) the copper foil on the inside of all the box pieces. Make sure there are no bumps of solder on the foil. It must be smooth to ensure an accurate fit.

9 Tack solder (p30) 2 of the bevels together at right angles, using the mirrored bottom piece as a guide. Repeat with the remaining 2 bevels.

10 Bring the 2 sections together and tack solder at the top and bottom of the adjoining edges, keeping the 4 sides square.

NOTE The appearance of a difference in height, at the points where the 2 halves meet, is merely an optical illusion.

11 Tack solder the mirrored bottom to the sides.

12 Tin all exposed seams, both inside and out.

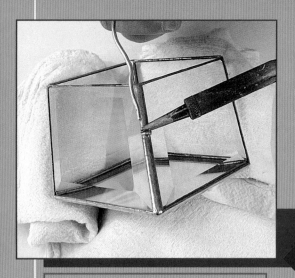

13 Bead solder (p30) the outside seams first, then the inside seams. By beading the outside seams first, some of the solder may drip through to the inside corners that the soldering iron tip may not be able to reach. The seams must be kept level to achieve an even solder seam. Prop the box with some cloths or use a cardboard box filled with crumpled newspaper.

14 Tin and bead solder the top edges of the box.

Making the Lid

15 Repeat the same steps used for the bottom. Check that lid fits over the bottom before bead soldering.

16 Clean (p33) the project.

17 Apply finishing compound or wax (p34).

60% OF ORIGINAL SIZE

SIZE OF ENLARGED PATTERNS IS
BASE   4 IN X 4 IN
LID   4-5/8 IN X 4-5/8 IN
BEVELS 4 IN X 7 IN
EACH SIDE OF BEVEL   4 IN

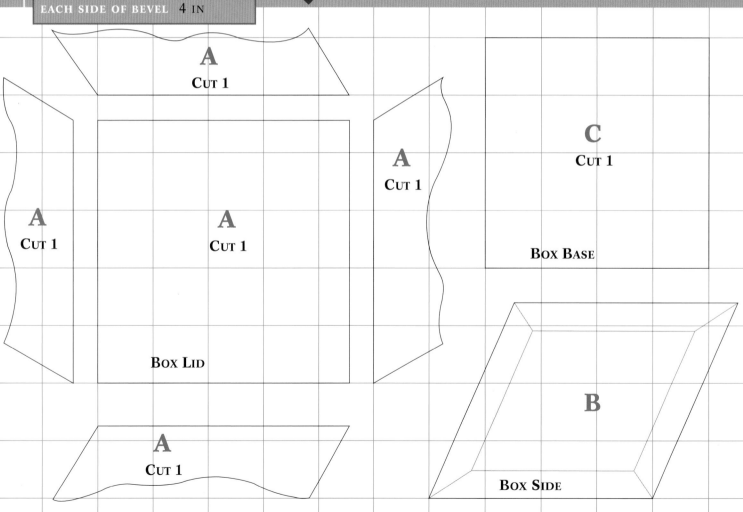

A
CUT 1

A
CUT 1

A
CUT 1

A
CUT 1

C
CUT 1

BOX BASE

A
CUT 1

BOX LID

B

BOX SIDE

A
CUT 1

DIAGONAL BOX AND LID PATTERN–1 SQUARE = 1 INCH

Vase #1

DIMENSIONS   6-1/2 in wide by 8-5/8 in high
NO. OF PIECES   18
NO. OF SIDES   4
GLASS REQUIRED

Letters refer to the type of glass used on pattern pieces (p102).

  A   12–4 in x 7 in clear diamond bevels
  B   1–4 in x 4 in 3mm mirror
  C   1–6 in x 10 in aqua craquel

This quantity of glass is the exact amount needed for the pattern. You may have to purchase more glass. Please allow for matching textures and grain.

MATERIALS
1 copy of pattern
Masking tape
Clear nail polish
Silver-backed and black-backed copper foil
Safety flux
60/40 solder
Cardboard box
Newspaper
Neutralizing solution
Black patina
Wax or finishing compound

TOOLS
Apron
Safety glasses
Utility knife or scissors
Permanent waterproof fine-tipped marker
Cork-backed straightedge
Glass cutter
Running pliers
Breaking pliers
Glass grinder
Soft cloths
Lathekin or doweling
Soldering iron and stand
Natural fiber sponge
Cotton swabs
Rubber gloves
Fine steel wool (000)
Toothbrush

Preparing the Pieces for Outer and Inner Vases

1   Prepare glass pieces for outer and inner vases following steps 1 to 7 of Diagonal Box and Lid (p97).

NOTE   Wrap each glass piece of the outer vase with silver-backed copper foil, crimp, and burnish (p29) down the edges. Wrap each glass piece of the inner vase with black-backed copper foil, crimp, and burnish down the edges.

Assembling the Outer Vase

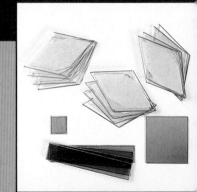

2   Tin (p30) the copper foil on the inside edges of all the clear bevels and the top side of the mirrored piece. Make sure there are no bumps of solder on the copper foil. It must be smooth to ensure an accurate fit.

3   Tack solder (p30) 2 of the bevels together at right angles, using the mirrored bottom piece as a guide. Repeat this step with the remaining bevels.

4   Bring 2 of the sections together and tack at the top and bottom of the adjoining seams, keeping the 4 sides square. Repeat this step with the other sections, creating 3–4-sided sections.

NOTE   The appearance of a difference in height at the points where the 2 sections meet is merely an optical illusion.

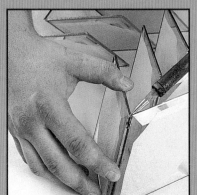

100

5 Positioning the mirrored bottom piece over the opening of one of the bevel sections, tack the base to the side pieces at several places.

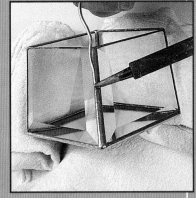

6 Tin all exposed copper foil seams, inside and outside of the base section created in step 5.

7 Bead solder (p30) the outside seams first and then the inside seams. By beading the outside seams first, some of the solder may melt through into the inside corners that the soldering iron tip may not be able to reach. The seams must be kept level to achieve an even solder seam. Prop the base section with some cloths or use a cardboard box filled with crumpled newspaper.

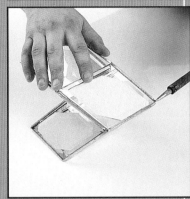

8 Wash the inside of the base section with clean water and neutralizing solution and dry with a soft cloth. Because of the shape of the outer vase, washing the base after each section is attached is recommended.

9 Position a second section of bevels onto the base section. The angle of the new section should be going in the opposite direction to that of the base section. Making sure the corners and edges of each section are aligned, tack solder the sections together.

10 Tin and bead solder the adjoining seams between the 2 sections as well as the side seams of the second section (inside and outside).

11 Wash the inside of the 2 sections with clean water and neutralizing solution. Dry with a clean cloth.

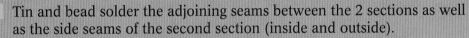

12 Attach the third section of bevels to the second section, using steps 9 and 10 as your guide.

13 Tin and bead solder the top edges of the vase.

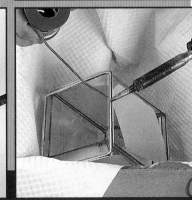

Assembling the Inner Vase

14 Tin the inside edges of the 4 side pieces and the base piece.

15 Bring together 2 side pieces to form a right angle, with the inside edges touching. Tack solder together.

16 Bring together and tack the 2 remaining side pieces, as above.

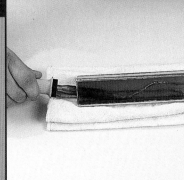

17 Bring the 2 halves together and tack at the top and bottom edges. Make sure that the vase is square.

18 Carefully tin and bead solder the inside and outside seams. Because of the narrowness of the vase, it can be difficult to touch up the solder on the inside seams if there is a melt-through.

101

19 ▶ Position the base on the bottom opening and tack into place.

20 ▶ Carefully tin and bead solder the adjoining seams to prevent melt-through.

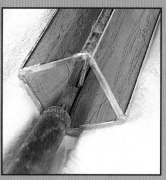  

21 Tin and bead solder the top edges of the vase.

22 Clean (p33) the 2 vases.

23 Apply patina (p33) to the inner vase only–the outer vase remains silver.

24 Apply finishing compound or wax (p34).

25 Place inner vase on mirrored bottom of outer vase. The 2 vases are not attached in any way.

75% OF ORIGINAL SIZE

SIZE OF ENLARGED PATTERNS IS
OUTER VASE BEVELS   4 IN X 7 IN
EACH SIDE OF BEVEL   4 IN
OUTER VASE BASE   4 IN X 4 IN
INNER VASE BASE 1-9/16 IN X 1-9/16 IN
INNER VASE SIDE   1-1/2 IN X 8 IN

VASE #1 PATTERN–1 SQUARE = 1 INCH

OUTER VASE SIDE

INNER VASE BASE

C
CUT 1

C
CUT 4

OUTER VASE BASE

A

B
CUT 1

INNER VASE SIDE

102

Vase #2

DIMENSIONS   7-3/16 in wide by 12-3/8 in high
by 3-3/8 in deep

NO. OF PIECES   15

GLASS REQUIRED

Letters refer to the type of glass used on pattern pieces (p106).

A   12 in x 20 in champagne/white/clear swirl
B   5 in x 6 in champagne pink cathedral
C   4 in x 11 in white/clear wispy
D   2–39mm champagne triangle faceted jewel

This quantity of glass is the exact amount needed for the pattern. You may have to purchase more glass. Please allow for matching textures and grain.

MATERIALS

2 copies of pattern
Wood board
Wood trim
Masking tape
Copper-backed copper foil
Safety flux
60/40 solder
Electrical tape
Cardboard box
Newspaper
Neutralizing solution
Copper patina
Wax or finishing compound

TOOLS

Apron
Safety glasses
Utility knife or scissors
Permanent waterproof fine-
tipped marker
Cork-backed straightedge
Glass cutter
Running pliers
Breaking pliers
Hammer and nails
Glass grinder
Soft cloths
Lathekin or doweling
Soldering iron and stand
Natural fiber sponge
Cotton swabs
Rubber gloves
Fine steel wool (000)
Toothbrush

Preparing the Pieces

1   Make 2 copies (p16) of the pattern (p106). Use one copy as a guide for cutting and breaking the glass pieces. Use the second copy for fitting and soldering the front and back panels together.

NOTE   If you are using opalescent glass, make a third pattern copy. Cut out the necessary pieces to use as a template, remembering to cut *inside* the pattern lines.

2   Using the marker, trace (p17) each pattern piece on the glass to be cut.

3   Cut (pp18–25) each piece of glass *inside* the marker line. Use a cork-backed straightedge to assist in scoring straight lines (p22).

4   Make a jig (p18) to fit together accurately the glass pieces for the front and back panels.

5   Grind (p26) each piece of glass to fit the pattern, leaving 1/32 in width between each piece so that the pattern line is clearly visible. Rinse each piece under clean water to remove any grinding residue and dry with a soft cloth.

6   Choose the width of copper foil (7/32 in is most common) appropriate for the thickness of glass you are using. Wrap each glass piece with copper foil, crimp, and burnish (p29) down the edges.

Assembling the Front and Back Panels

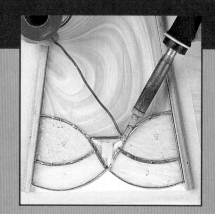

7   Arrange the foiled pieces for the front panel on the pattern in the jig and tack solder (p30) the pieces together.

8   Tin (p30) all exposed copper foil seams.

9   Bead solder (p30) all the seams on the panel. Turn the panel over and repeat the soldering procedure. On the back side of the panel, leave 1/4 in of the solder seams (that intersect with the sides of the panel) free of solder.

10 Repeat steps 7 to 9 to assemble the back panel of the vase.

 11 Tin the exposed copper foil on the 2 side pieces and the base piece only on the sides that will be facing the interior of the vase.

Assembling the Vase

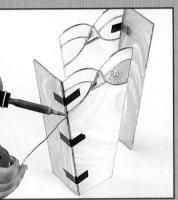 

12 Bring together the front panel and a side piece so the inside edges touch and are at a right angle to each other. Use electrical tape to hold the 2 panels together. Tack solder together.

13 Bring together and tack the remaining side piece and the back panel, as above.

14 Bring the 2 halves together and tack at the bottom and top edges.

15 Turn the vase upside down and position the base piece on the bottom opening. Make sure the vase is square. Tack solder the base to the rest of the vase.

16 Tin all exposed copper foil on the exterior of vase.

17 Fill a cardboard box with crumpled newspaper to hold the vase at the appropriate angle for soldering.

18 Placing the vase inside the cardboard box, tin and bead solder the interior seams of the vase. Be sure to bead solder the unsoldered seam edges on the inside of the front and back panels now that the vase has been assembled. Keep the seams level as they are being soldered.

19 Bead solder the exterior seams.

20 Tin and bead solder the top edges of the vase.

21 Clean (p33) the vase.

22 Apply patina (p33).

 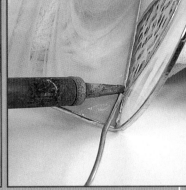

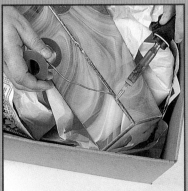 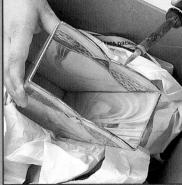

23 Apply finishing compound or wax (p34).

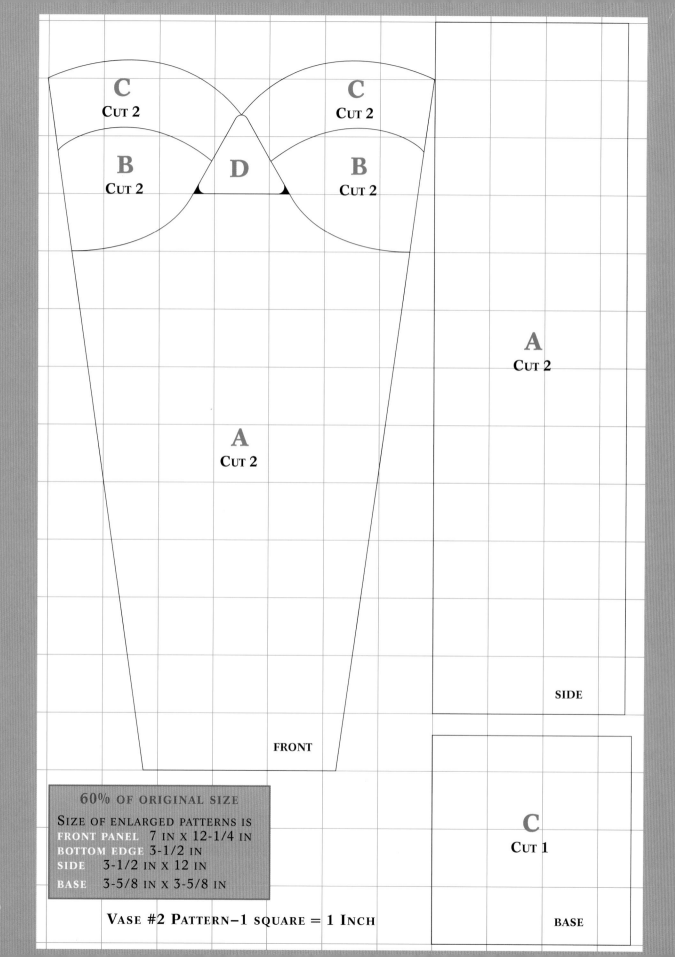

C
CUT 2

C
CUT 2

B
CUT 2

D

B
CUT 2

A
CUT 2

A
CUT 2

SIDE

C
CUT 1

BASE

FRONT

60% OF ORIGINAL SIZE

SIZE OF ENLARGED PATTERNS IS
FRONT PANEL   7 IN X 12-1/4 IN
BOTTOM EDGE 3-1/2 IN
SIDE   3-1/2 IN X 12 IN
BASE   3-5/8 IN X 3-5/8 IN

VASE #2 PATTERN—1 SQUARE = 1 INCH

Vase #3

DIMENSIONS 9-1/16 in high

NO. OF PIECES 16

GLASS REQUIRED

Letters refer to the type of glass used on pattern pieces (p110).

    A 7 in x 9 in iridescent black opal

    B 9 in x 18 in black opal

    C 6–iridescent black marbles

This quantity of glass is the exact amount needed for the pattern. You may have to purchase more glass. Please allow for matching textures and grain.

MATERIALS

2 copies of pattern
Wood board
Wood trim
Masking tape
Copper-backed copper foil
Safety flux
60/40 solder
Electrical tape
Cardboard box
Newspaper
Neutralizing solution
Black patina
Wax or finishing compound

TOOLS

Apron
Safety glasses
Utility knife or scissors
Permanent waterproof fine-
   tipped marker
Cork-backed straightedge
Glass cutter
Running pliers
Breaking pliers
Hammer and nails
Glass grinder
1/4 in drilling/grinding bit
Soft cloths
Lathekin or doweling
Soldering iron and stand
Natural fiber sponge
Cotton swabs
8 pennies
Rubber gloves
Fine steel wool (000)
Toothbrush

Preparing the Pieces

1 Follow steps 1 to 6 for Vase #2 (p104).

NOTE Grind (p26) and fit the pieces for one panel at a time, labeling each set with a marker. The shaded areas on the pattern are to be ground out with the 1/4 in drilling/grinding bit, leaving space for placing the marbles.

2 Wrap the marbles with 7/32 in copper foil. The foil must be centered and burnished (p29) to the surface of each marble.

Assembling the Pieces

3 Arrange the foiled pieces for the first panel on the pattern in the jig and tack solder (p30) the pieces together. Do not tack the marbles in place at this time.

4 Follow steps 8 to 10 for Vase #2 ([104).

5 Stack the pennies in 4 rows of 2 on the pattern. Place the panel on top of the pennies, making sure that they are positioned so that the panel is properly supported and level. The pennies should be in contact with the glass and not a solder seam.

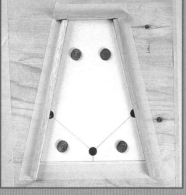

6 Place a marble in the center opening so the foil around the marble is in contact with the foil around the opening. Tack into place and proceed to tin and bead solder the seam around the marble on both sides of the panel.

7 Repeat steps 3 to 6 for each of the 3 panels.

8 With a damp cloth, wipe the excess flux off the panels and dry with a soft cloth.

9 Lay the panels side by side on the work surface with the side edges touching. Align the panels so that the top and bottom edges as well as any adjoining seams match up.

 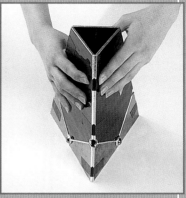

10 Cut 9 pieces of electrical tape in 3 in strips. Tape the adjoining panels together in 3 locations.

NOTE   Use only electrical tape for this stage of construction.

11 Pull the panels up into a 3-sided cone shape by slowly lifting the top edges of the panels and matching the inside edges of the 2 end panels together, top and bottom. Using the remaining 3 pieces of electrical tape, join the 2 end panels together.

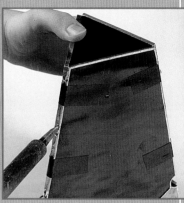

12 Tack solder each adjoining edge together in several locations.

13 Tin the copper foil on the base piece making sure there are no bumps of solder on the foil. Position the base piece on the bottom opening. Tack solder the base to the rest of the vase.

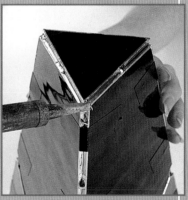

14 Fill a cardboard box with crumpled newspaper to hold the vase at the appropriate angle for soldering. Place the vase inside the box, positioning it so that one of the outside seams is level and facing skyward.

15 Place a marble into the open space located on the seam. The marble should be positioned so the copper foil runs in the same direction as the seam. Tack solder into place. Repeat procedure with the 2 remaining sides.

16 Tin and bead solder all exposed copper foil seams, inside and out. Be sure to bead solder the unsoldered seam edges on the inside of the panels. Keep the seams level as they are being soldered.

17 Tin and bead solder the top edges of the vase.

18 Clean (p33) the vase.

19 Apply patina (p33).

20 Apply finishing compound or wax (p34).

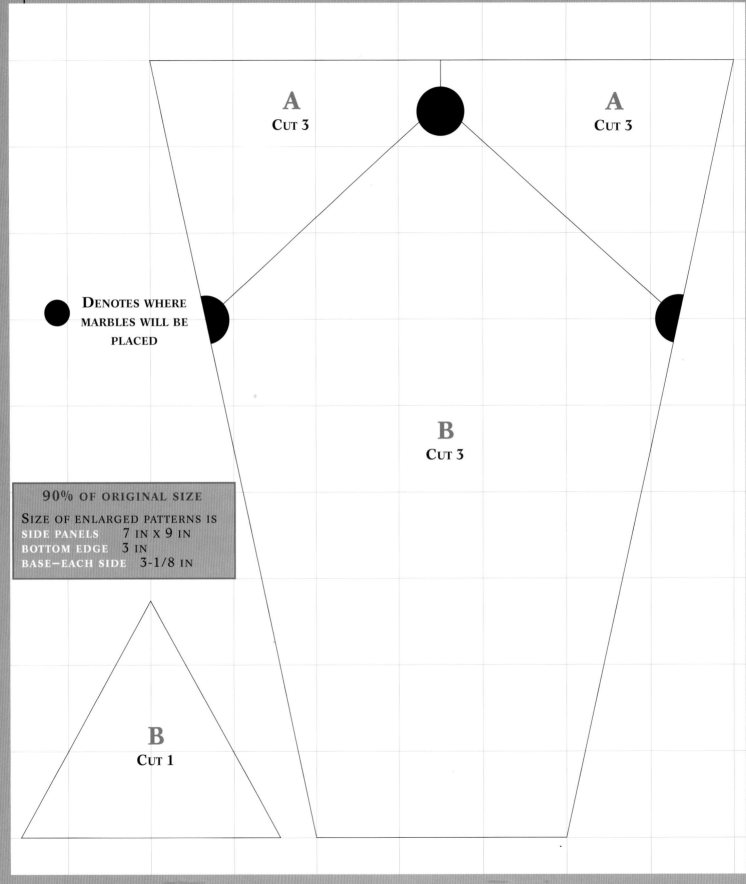

A
CUT 3

A
CUT 3

DENOTES WHERE
MARBLES WILL BE
PLACED

B
CUT 3

90% OF ORIGINAL SIZE

SIZE OF ENLARGED PATTERNS IS
SIDE PANELS   7 IN X 9 IN
BOTTOM EDGE   3 IN
BASE—EACH SIDE   3-1/8 IN

B
CUT 1

VASE #3 PATTERN–1 SQUARE = 1 INCH

Candleholder Set

DIMENSIONS each holder diameter 4 in
NO. OF PIECES 33
GLASS REQUIRED

Letters refer to the type of glass used on pattern pieces (p114–5).

A	5 in x 18 in blue craquel
B	5 in x 14 in 3mm mirror
C	3–1 in x 2 in clear bevels
D	3–1 in x 3 in clear bevels
E	5–1 in x 4 in clear bevels
F	4–1 in x 5 in clear bevels

This quantity of glass is the exact amount needed for the pattern. You may have to purchase more glass. Please allow for matching textures and grain.

MATERIALS
1 copy of pattern
1/8 in single channel U-
  shaped lead came
Safety flux
60/40 solder
Silver-backed copper foil
Electrical tape
Cardboard box
Newspaper
Neutralizing solution
Wax or finishing compound
3 votive cups and tea lights

TOOLS
Apron
Safety glasses
Permanent waterproof fine-
  tipped marker
Cork-backed straightedge
Glass cutter
Running pliers
Breaking pliers
Glass grinder
Soft cloths
Lead vise
Lead knippers
Soldering iron and stand
Natural fiber sponge
Cotton swabs
Lathekin or doweling
Utility knife or scissors
Toothbrush

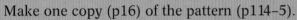

Preparing the Pieces

1 Make one copy (p16) of the pattern (p114–5).

NOTE If you are using opalescent glass, make a second pattern copy. Cut out the necessary pieces to use as a template, remembering to cut inside the pattern lines.

2 Trace (p16) and cut (pp18–25) the pieces of blue craquel and mirror, making sure to cut *inside* the pattern lines. Use the cork-backed straightedge to assist in scoring straight lines (p22).

NOTE *See* How to Prepare Mirrored Glass (p28).

3 Grind (p26) each piece of glass to fit the pattern. Bevel mirror pieces (p28).

NOTE This pattern uses clear bevels and a mirror. Verify that the bevels fit the pattern and grind to fit if they do not (p28).

Making the Candle Holder Bases

4 To stretch lead came to eliminate any slack or kinks, follow steps 6 and 7 of Thistle Hanging Panel (p51).

5 Using the lead knippers, cut 3–13 in lengths of lead. Wrap each mirror base with the came, cutting off any excess with a pair of lead knippers. Have the channeling facing skyward and cut with the flat side of the lead knippers facing away from the excess lead. The trimmed ends of the came should be butted together.

6 Tack solder (p30) the ends of the lead came together. The tack should not be bulging but should be as close to the surface of the lead as possible.

Making the Candleholder Sides

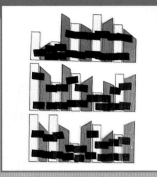

7 Using 7/32 in copper foil, wrap each piece of blue craquel and all the bevels. Crimp and burnish (p29) down the edges.

8 Arrange the pieces as indicated on the pattern, making sure the bottom edges of the pieces line up evenly and there is a 1/16 in space between each piece. Using small strips of electrical tape, join the pieces together.

NOTE   Use only electrical tape for this stage of construction.

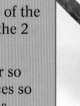

9 Pull the pieces up into a cylindrical shape by slowly lifting the top edges of the end pieces and matching both the top and bottom edges together. Tape the 2 end pieces together, forming a cylindrical shape.

10 Place the cylinder onto a mirrored base, and carefully shape the cylinder so that the pieces will rest on the mirror, not the lead came. Shape the pieces so that as many joints will be touching the inside of the lead came border as possible. You may have to make a few adjustments to the pieces that will be used on the 2 mirror bases that have the small inside curve. Tack the pieces together in several places with solder but do not tack to the base.

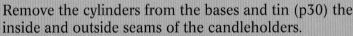

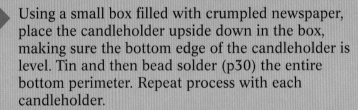

11 Remove the cylinders from the bases and tin (p30) the inside and outside seams of the candleholders.

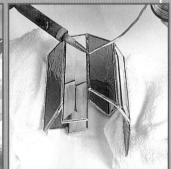

12 Using a small box filled with crumpled newspaper, place the candleholder upside down in the box, making sure the bottom edge of the candleholder is level. Tin and then bead solder (p30) the entire bottom perimeter. Repeat process with each candleholder.

13 Lay the candleholder on its side on the work surface and bead solder the inside and outside seams. Use old cloths to prop the candleholder so that the cylinder does not move. Repeat process with each candleholder.

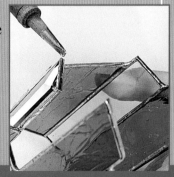

14 Tin and bead solder the top edges of each candleholder—let the solder cool before turning the project to bead the next edge.

15 Wash off excess flux with clean water and neutralizing solution. Dry with a soft cloth.

Attaching the Side to the Base

16 Place each candleholder onto the corresponding base. Tack solder each seam of the candleholder to the lead came around the mirror base. In order for the candleholder set to fit together properly avoid getting solder on the outside edge of the lead came.

17 Once the candleholder has been securely tacked to the base, bead solder each tack and the adjoining seam, achieving an even solder joint between the base and the candleholder. Repeat procedure with each candleholder.

18 Clean (p33) the project.

19 Apply finishing compound or wax (p34).

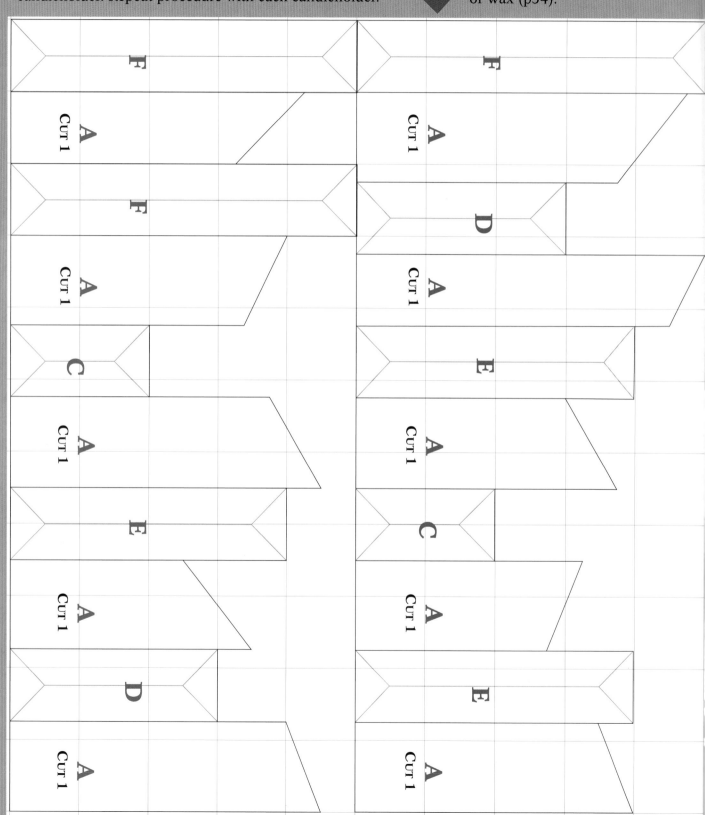

114

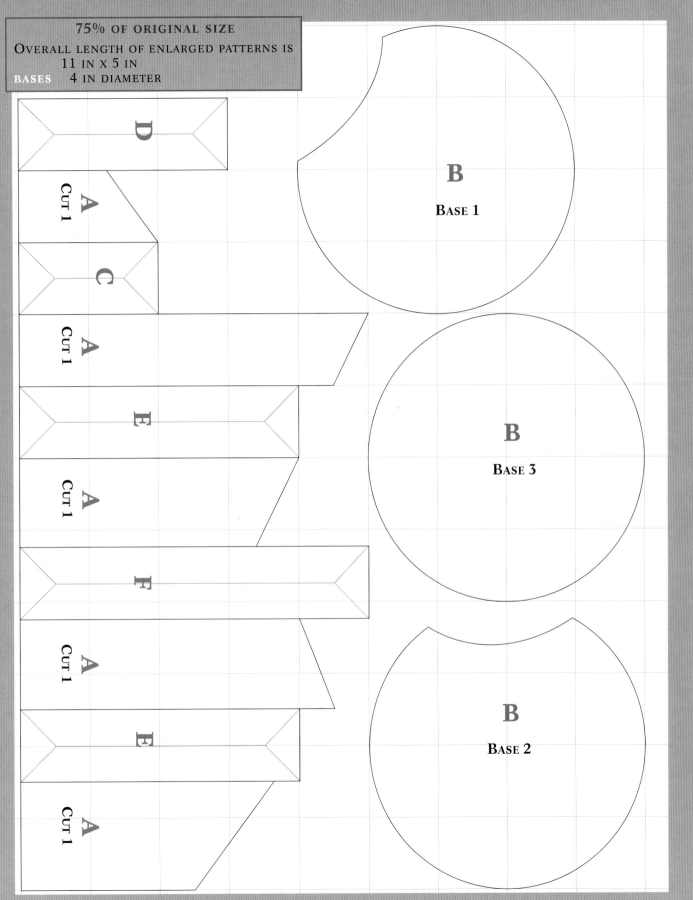

75% OF ORIGINAL SIZE
OVERALL LENGTH OF ENLARGED PATTERNS IS
11 IN X 5 IN
BASES   4 IN DIAMETER

D

CUT 1 A

C

CUT 1 A

E

CUT 1 A

F

CUT 1 A

E

CUT 1 A

B
BASE 1

B
BASE 3

B
BASE 2

CANDLEHOLDER SET PATTERN–1 SQUARE = 1 INCH

115

DIMENSIONS   8-1/4 in wide by 6 in high
                 by 7-1/4 in deep

NO. OF PIECES   9

GLASS REQUIRED

Letters refer to the type of glass used on pattern pieces (pp118–9).

A   1–5-1/2 in x 14-1/2 in iridescent black opal

B   1–4 in x 6 in black opal

C   4–iridescent black marbles

This quantity of glass is the exact amount needed for the pattern. You may have to purchase more glass. Please allow for matching textures and grain.

MATERIALS

2 copies of pattern
Wood board
Wood trim
Masking tape
Copper-backed copper foil
Safety flux
60/40 solder
Cardboard box
Newspaper
Neutralizing solution
Black patina
Wax or finishing compound
Clock movement *(available in various sizes at most hobby/craft shops)*

TOOLS

Apron
Safety glasses
Utility knife or scissors
Permanent waterproof fine-
    tipped marker
Cork-backed straightedge
Glass cutter
Running pliers
Breaking pliers
Hammer and nails
Glass grinder
1/4 in drilling/grinding bit
Soft cloths
Lathekin or doweling
Soldering iron and stand
Natural fiber sponge
Cotton swabs
Rubber gloves
Fine steel wool (000)
Toothbrush

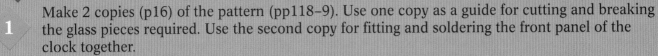

Preparing the Pieces

1 Make 2 copies (p16) of the pattern (pp118–9). Use one copy as a guide for cutting and breaking the glass pieces required. Use the second copy for fitting and soldering the front panel of the clock together.

NOTE If you are using opalescent glass, make a third copy and cut out the necessary pattern pieces to use as a template, remembering to cut *inside* the pattern lines.

2 Using the marker, trace (p17) each pattern piece on the glass to be cut. Place the pattern pieces so that the texture and grain of the glass are taken into account.

3 Cut (pp18–23) each piece of glass *inside* the marker line. Use the cork-backed straightedge to assist in scoring straight lines (p22).

4 Make a jig (p18) to help fit the glass pieces for the front panel of the clock together accurately.

5 Grind (p26) each piece of glass to fit the pattern. For the front panel leave 1/32 in width between each piece so that the pattern line is clearly visible. Rinse each piece under clean water to remove any grinding residue. Dry with a soft cloth.

NOTE The black areas on the pattern indicate the placement of the marbles. Grind out (p27) these areas with the 1/4 in drilling/grinding bit, leaving a space for the marbles. Also, drill a hole (p27) into the center of black piece B of glass for the shaft of the clock movement. Check that the shaft fits through the opening. If not, grind to the size required.

6 Choose the width of copper foil (7/32 in is most common) appropriate for the thickness of the glass you are using. Wrap each glass piece with the copper foil, crimp, and burnish (p29) down the edges.

7 Wrap the marbles with 7/32 in copper foil. The foil must be centered and burnished to the surface of each marble.

Assembling the Front Panel

8 Arrange the foiled pieces for the front panel onto the pattern in the jig and tack solder (p30) the pieces together. Do not tack the marbles into place at this time.

9 Tin (p30) all exposed copper foil seams.

10 Bead solder (p30) all the seams on the panel. Turn the panel over and repeat the soldering procedure. On the back side of the panel, leave 1/4 in of the solder seams that intersect with the sides of the panel, free of solder.

11 Tin the exposed copper foil along the edges of the undersides of the front panel and the side pieces. Make sure there are no bumps of solder on the copper foil. It must be smooth to ensure an accurate fit.

12 With a damp cloth, wipe the excess flux off the panel and dry with a soft cloth.

13 Lay the front panel and the side pieces on the work surface matching up the side edges. Align the top and bottom edges.

14 Cut 9–2 in strips of electrical tape. Tape the front panel and adjoining side pieces together in 3 locations.

NOTE   Use only electrical tape for this stage of construction.

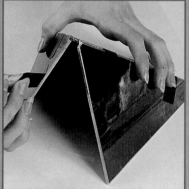

15 Pull the panel and side pieces up into a 3-sided cone shape by slowly lifting the top edges and matching the inside edges of the 2 side pieces together, top and bottom. Using the remaining 3 pieces of electrical tape, join the 2 side pieces together.

16 Tack solder each adjoining edge together in several locations.

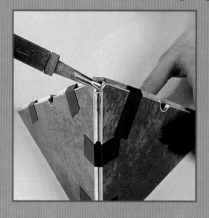

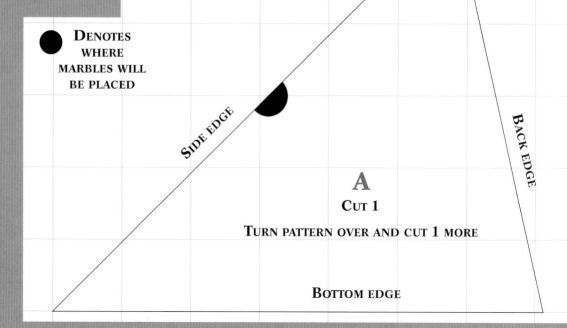

75% OF ORIGINAL SIZE

SIZE OF ENLARGED PATTERN IS
BOTTOM EDGE   7-1/8 IN
BACK EDGE   5-1/2 IN
SIDE EDGE   7-13/16 IN

SIDE PANEL

● DENOTES WHERE MARBLES WILL BE PLACED

SIDE EDGE

BACK EDGE

A

CUT 1

TURN PATTERN OVER AND CUT 1 MORE

BOTTOM EDGE

17 Fill a cardboard box with crumpled newspaper to hold the clock at the appropriate angle for soldering. Place the clock inside the box, positioning it so one of the adjoining seams is level and facing skyward.

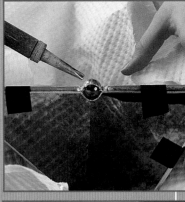

18 Place a marble into the open space located on the seam. The marble should be positioned so that the copper foil runs in the same direction as the seam. Tack solder in place.

19 Tack remaining marbles in place. Make sure that the copper foil around the opening on the front panel is aligned with the foil around the marble.

20 Tin and bead solder all inside and outside seams and around the marbles.

21 Tin and bead solder the bottom edge of the clock, making sure to place a generous bead of solder on the inside bottom corners for additional support.

22 Clean (p33) the project.

23 Apply patina (p33).

24 Apply finishing compound or wax (p34).

25 Install clock movement, following manufacturer's instructions.

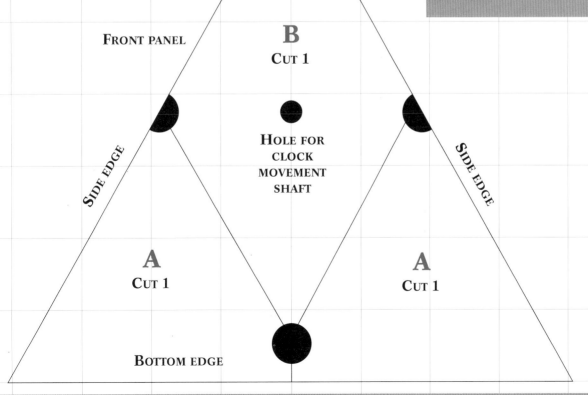

75% OF ORIGINAL SIZE

SIZE OF ENLARGED PATTERN IS
BOTTOM EDGE   8-1/8 IN
SIDE EDGES   7-13/16 IN

FRONT PANEL

B
CUT 1

HOLE FOR CLOCK MOVEMENT SHAFT

SIDE EDGE

SIDE EDGE

A
CUT 1

A
CUT 1

BOTTOM EDGE

DESK CLOCK PATTERN–1 SQUARE = 1 INCH

Sand Garden

DIMENSIONS 12-1/8 in wide by 12-3/16 in high by 7 in deep

NO. OF PIECES 42

GLASS REQUIRED

Letters refer to the type of glass used on pattern pieces (pp125–7).

A 1–14 in x 17-1/4 in clear semi antique
B 1–12 in x 12 in 3mm mirror
C 1–6 in x 12 in black opal

This quantity of glass is the exact amount needed for the pattern. You may have to purchase more glass. Please allow for matching textures and grain.

MATERIALS
2 copies of pattern
Wood board
Wood trim
Masking tape
Clear nail polish
1/4 in copper-backed copper foil
1/2 in copper-backed copper foil
Safety flux
60/40 solder
Cardboard box
Newspaper
3 rod and tube hinge assemblies
22 in fine-linked chain
Neutralizing solution
Copper patina
Wax or finishing compound
Silica sand and marbles

TOOLS
Apron
Safety glasses
Utility knife or scissors
Permanent waterproof fine-tipped marker
Cork-backed straightedge
Glass cutter
Running pliers
Breaking pliers
Hammer and nails
Glass grinder
Soft cloths
Lathekin or doweling
Soldering iron and stand
Natural fiber sponge
Cotton swabs
Small file
Wooden toothpicks
Sidecutters or lead knippers
Needle-nose pliers
Rubber gloves
Fine steel wool (000)
Toothbrush

Preparing the Pieces

1. Make 2 copies (p16) of the pattern (pp125–7). Use one copy as a guide for cutting and breaking the glass pieces required. Use the second copy for fitting and soldering the lid and front panels together.

   NOTE If you are using opalescent glass, make a third copy and cut out the necessary pattern pieces to use as a template, remembering to cut *inside* the pattern lines.

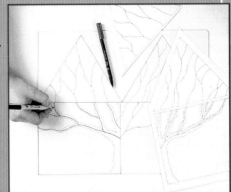

2. Using the marker, trace (p17) base outline onto black opal glass; back panel outline onto mirrored glass; and lid and front panels outline onto the sheet of clear semi-antique glass. Trace the cutting lines (the solid lines) onto each lid and front panel.

3. Cut (pp18–25) the base and back pieces. Use the cork-backed straightedge to assist in scoring straight lines (p22).

4. Cut the sheet of clear semi-antique glass into the 4 panels and proceed to cut out the individual pieces of glass. The panels have been designed so that the pieces in each panel can be cut out without any waste.

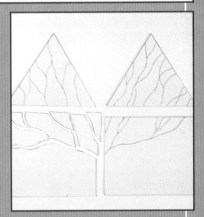

5. Each lid and front panel requires its own jig (p18) to help fit the individual glass pieces together accurately and to keep the panels the correct size and shape.

6. Grind (p26) each piece as required to fit the pattern.

7. Prepare the mirror back piece (p28).

Instructions for Foiling the Sand Garden

8. Wrap the base, the mirror back piece, and the lid panel pieces with 1/4 in copper foil. Crimp and burnish (p29) down the edges.

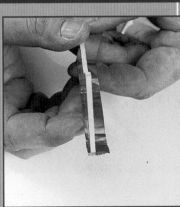

9. A thicker copper foil is needed to achieve the tree branch effect on the lower panels. Some pieces will require the application of 2 different widths of foil.
   This is how to do it.
   a) Wrap each piece (only the edges that are along the inside seams) with 1/2 in copper foil. Position the copper foil so that there is a greater overlap onto the front of the glass than on the back.
   b) Any portion of a glass piece that is part of the top edge, the bottom seam, or the outside seam (adjacent to the mirror back piece), must be wrapped with 1/4 in copper foil. Wrap the foil along the edge and over onto the interior seam edges about 1/4 in. This will ensure that the copper foil does not lift when you are bead soldering the top edge and the outside seam.

c) If tears develop along the curves, overlap the tears with copper foil and burnish.

10 Create the tree trunk with copper foil overlay. Using the pattern as a reference, apply enough copper foil on the topside of the glass to cover the trunk area (and any branch that requires a bit more thickness). Lay the 1/2 in copper foil onto the glass in approximately 3 rows, overlapping slightly on the adjacent row. Burnish firmly to the glass.

11 Using the dotted lines on the pattern as a reference, mark the outline of the branches and trunk onto the copper foil. Cut away the excess copper foil with a utility knife (use a new blade). Take care when cutting that you do not press too hard with the knife and create a score line on the glass.

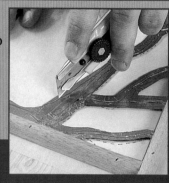

12 Trim away any foil on the underside of the glass that you do not wish to see from the front.

Assembling the Lid Panels

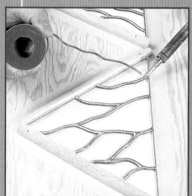

13 Arrange the foiled pieces for one of the lid panels on the pattern in the jig. Tack solder (p30) together.

14 Tin (p30) and bead solder (p30) the interior copper foiled seams together.

15 Turn the panel over and repeat step 14.

16 Tin the copper foil on the outside edges of the panel, both front and back. Proceed to bead solder the 2 side edges of the panel. Do not bead solder the bottom edge of the panel. This is the edge that the hinge will be soldered to.

17 Repeat steps 13 to 16 to assemble the second lid panel.

Assembling the Front Panels

18 For each of the front panels, follow steps 13 to 15. On the back side of the panels, leave 1/4 in of the solder seams (that intersects with the outside edges) free of solder.

NOTE   There will be a fair amount of molten solder placed on these panels to cover the copper foil overlay on the glass. Let the areas cool occasionally to prevent heat cracks. The bead soldering doesn't need to be perfect because a decorative soldering technique will be used to give the tree branches and the trunk a rough, bark-like texture.

19 ▸ Tin and bead solder the exposed copper foil along the top edge of each panel, remembering to keep approximately 1/4 in from each outside edge free of solder.

Attaching Front Panels to Base and Back Pieces

20 Bring together the 2 front panels so that the 2 inside edges are touching. Use the base piece as a guide to determine the correct angle. Tack solder together at several locations, leaving the top 2 in of the adjoining seam free of solder (for the rods of the hinge assemblies).

21 Tin the exposed copper foil on the base and the mirror back piece as well as along the interior edges of the 2 front panels. Make sure there are no bumps of solder on the copper foil. It must be smooth to ensure an accurate fit.

22 Align the outside edges of the mirror back piece with the outside edge of each of the front panels. Tack solder the panels and back piece together in several locations, leaving the top 2 in of the adjoining seams free of solder (for the rods of the hinge assemblies).

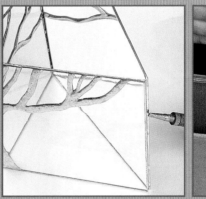

23 Position the sand garden onto the base piece and tack solder into place.

24 Fill a cardboard box with crumpled newspaper to hold the sand garden in the box and proceed to tin and bead solder all the inside and outside adjoining seams. Remember to leave the top 2 in on the adjoining seams free of solder.

25 Tin and bead solder the top 2 edges of the mirror back piece.

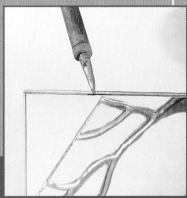

Attaching the Hinge Assemblies

26 ▸ Follow steps 23 to 28 of Hinged Box #1 (p88).
NOTE   Use one rod and tube hinge assembly for each lid panel.
NOTE For this project, the tube length is 8-1/8 in and each rod length is 4 in.

27 ▸ Remove the toothpicks and set a rod piece into the ends of the tube on each lid panel.

28 Lay a couple of sheets of scrap paper over the top edges of the 2 front panels on the sand garden.

29 Position the lid panels into place, aligning the panels with the mirror back piece and the front solder seam on the lower portion of the sand garden. The lid panels should be as close together as possible without impeding their movement or overlapping one another. Insert the rods into the corresponding open seams and tape the panels into place.

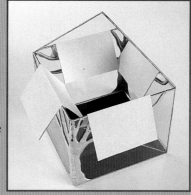 

30 Tack solder the rods at each seam. Remove the paper and ensure the freedom of movement of each lid panel, with as little gap between the lid panels and the lower front panels as possible.

31 Bead solder the rods in place, finishing the solder seams. (*See* step 31 of Hinged Box #1, p88).

Attaching the Chain

32 Leaving the rod inside the remaining hinge assembly, tin the outside of the tube and solder over each end so that the rod cannot come out of the tube. Allow to cool.

 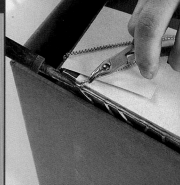

33 Position the tube across the back of the sand garden and tape into place at the same height as the point where the front lower panels and the lid panels meet. Solder the tube securely to each of the outside solder seams.

34 Place a piece of scrap paper between each lid panel and the mirror back piece. Holding one end of the fine-link chain with a pair of needle-nose pliers, tack solder the chain securely to one of the lid panels at the point where the topmost "branch" seam intersects with the outside edge. It should be positioned on the edge so that it will hang along the back of the sand garden and will not be visible from the front of the panel.

35 Repeat the above procedure, soldering the other end of the chain to the same position on the other lid panel.

36 Letting the chain hang freely down the back of the sand garden, mark the chain at its lowest point with the marker. Place a mark at the center of the tube running across the back of the sand garden.

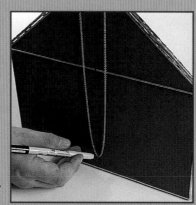 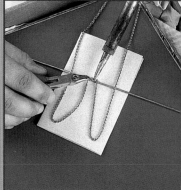

37 Place scrap paper between the mirror back piece and the tube running across it. This will prevent damage to the silvering or the possibility of a heat crack. Holding the chain with the needle-nose pliers, align the mark on the chain with the mark on the tube and solder the chain securely in place.

124

Decorative Soldering

38 To make the rough texture on the trunk and branches, start with solder seams that have been cooled. Apply flux sparingly to the solder and touch seam with the hot soldering iron tip. Leave the iron tip on the solder only long enough for the solder to start to melt. Raise the tip off the solder, leaving a dimple in the seam. Repeat the procedure until the desired effect is achieved.

39 Clean (p33) the project.

40 Apply copper patina (p33).

41 Apply finishing compound or wax (p34).

42 To create a sand garden, fill with silica sand and arrange marbles and found objects inside.

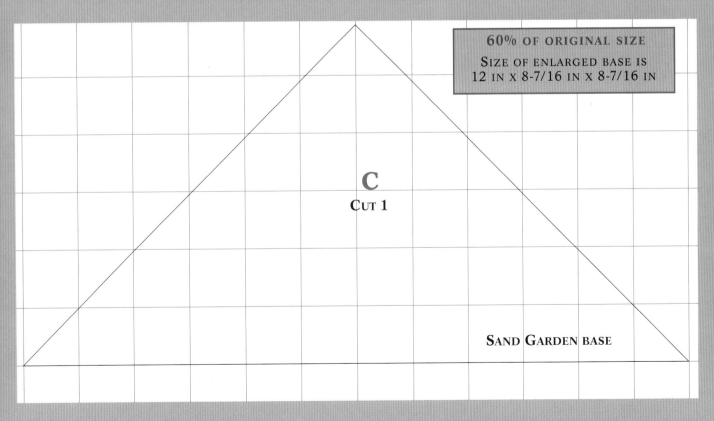

60% OF ORIGINAL SIZE

SIZE OF ENLARGED BASE IS 12 IN X 8-7/16 IN X 8-7/16 IN

C

CUT 1

SAND GARDEN BASE

SAND GARDEN PATTERN—1 SQUARE = 1 INCH

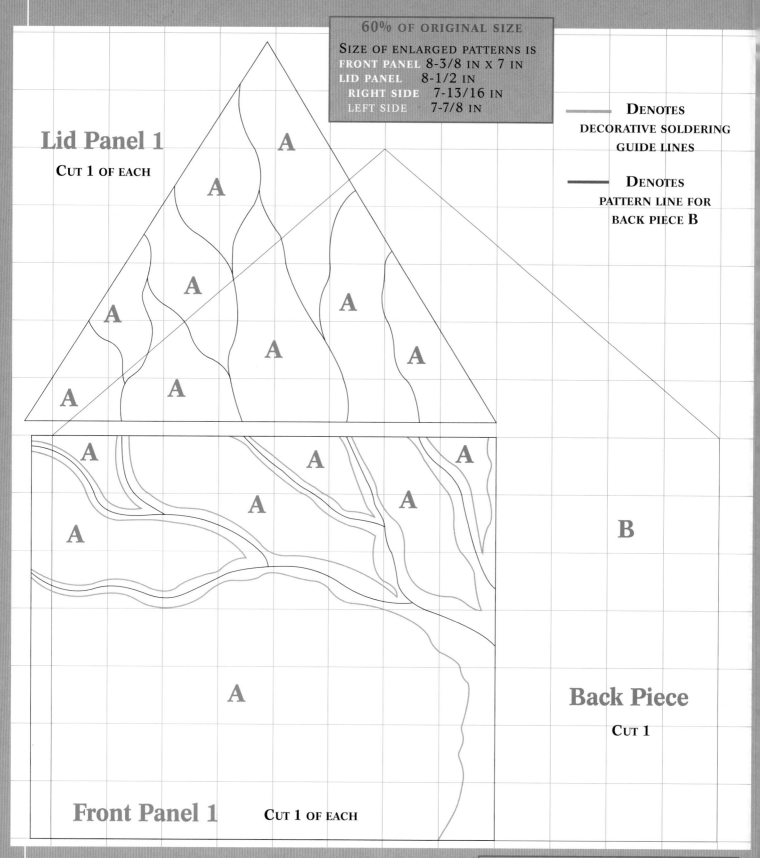

60% OF ORIGINAL SIZE

SIZE OF ENLARGED PATTERNS IS
FRONT PANEL 8-3/8 IN X 7 IN
LID PANEL   8-1/2 IN
  RIGHT SIDE   7-13/16 IN
  LEFT SIDE   7-7/8 IN

DENOTES
DECORATIVE SOLDERING
GUIDE LINES

DENOTES
PATTERN LINE FOR
BACK PIECE **B**

Lid Panel 1

CUT 1 OF EACH

A A A A A A A A A

Front Panel 1   CUT 1 OF EACH

A A A A A A A A

B

Back Piece

CUT 1

SAND GARDEN PATTERN–1 SQUARE = 1 INCH

SIZE OF ENLARGED BACK PIECE IS
12 IN X 12 IN AND EACH SIDE IS 7 IN

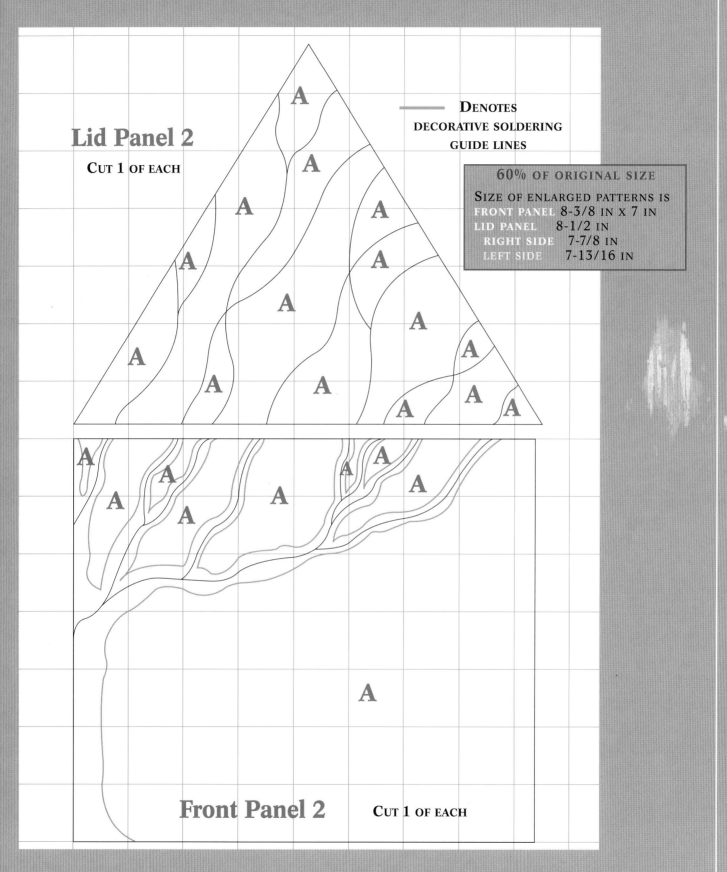

Lid Panel 2

CUT 1 OF EACH

——— DENOTES
DECORATIVE SOLDERING
GUIDE LINES

60% OF ORIGINAL SIZE

SIZE OF ENLARGED PATTERNS IS
FRONT PANEL 8-3/8 IN X 7 IN
LID PANEL   8-1/2 IN
RIGHT SIDE   7-7/8 IN
LEFT SIDE   7-13/16 IN

Front Panel 2   CUT 1 OF EACH

SAND GARDEN PATTERN–1 SQUARE = 1 INCH

Index